TRUTHS FOR BELIEVERS

Truths for Believers

Expositions
and Meditations on
Scriptural Subjects

Henry Dyer
Henry Heath
Henry Groves

JOHN RITCHIE LTD
CHRISTIAN PUBLICATIONS

40 Beansburn, Kilmarnock, Scotland

ISBN-13: 978 1 910513 29 3

Whilst every effort has been made to maintain a high quality of print in all of our publications, difficulties do arise in some instances. Where the book is printed from a scan of an older copy, there will be occasions where the print quality is not to our usual high standard. We apologise should you find any examples of this in this volume.

Typeset by John Ritchie Ltd., Kilmarnock
Printed by Bell & Bain Ltd., Glasgow

Contents

PART 3 - PATHS OF RIGHTEOUSNESS

Henry Groves

GREEN PASTURES,

FOR THE FLOCK OF GOD.

⸻ ✦❖✦ ⸻

"The Sufferings" and "The Glories."

⸻

THE apostle Peter speaks (1 Peter i. 11) of "the sufferings of Christ, and the glories that should follow," as the great theme of the testimony of "the Spirit of Christ," whether in the prophets of old, or the apostles now ; and we may well say—

> "Our song, then, for ever shall be
> Of the Shepherd who gave Himself thus ;
> No subject so glorious we see,
> And none so affecting to us."

The expression "gave Himself" brings to mind four principal aspects of the death of Christ, which have glories corresponding to them which will be His at His coming and in His kingdom. Each of these virtues of His death is denied by Satan, and by man in his unbelief.

The first of the four aspects is unfolded in Galatians ii. 20 : " Who loved *me*, and GAVE HIM-SELF for *me*."

B

The death of Jesus for the *individual sinner* is
here brought before us. Paul claims that death
as being for him, as distinctly and individually as
though it had been for him only. Each guilty
sinner needs, and must have, a *personal* Surety, a
living Substitute; and JESUS only can be this for
any one. Quite true that others claim Him as well
as Paul—that every sinner ever saved through Him
thus claims Him; still, it remains blessedly true,
that Jesus *Himself* died on the cross as the Substitute for the individual sinner. Reason cannot explain
this; but God declares, and faith owns, that while
Jesus was the Substitute for one transgressor, He
was also at the same time the Substitute for all
others who trust in Him. Nothing short of an
entire person would do for each individual sinner.
Nothing short of the whole Lamb, and that "the
Lamb of God," could save any single sinner from
the depth of a bottomless hell, or raise him to the
bosom of the infinitely and eternally blessed God.
Jesus, therefore, died on the cross as the Substitute
for the individual sinner.

But a second aspect of the cross appears: Jesus
died there as the lover of the Church, given Him
of the Father (see Ephesians v. 25). "Christ also
loved the *Church*, and GAVE HIMSELF for *it*, that
He might sanctify and cleanse *it* . . . that He
might present *it* to Himself a glorious Church," &c.

His eye of love and of compassion beheld this
precious object in its unsanctified and uncleansed

state, and He gave Himself in death to make it His.   Like Samson, in Judges xiv., who saw " the daughter of the Philistines," and out of love to her, faced the roaring lion, and, with " nothing in his hand, rent him as he would have rent a kid," so Jesus, in willingness of *love*, " gave Himself " for the Church to make it His for ever.   This is a second aspect of His death.

But there is a third : He died at the cross as *God's appointed King.*

" Art thou a King, then?" said Pilate to Him (John xviii. 37).   " Jesus answered, Thou sayest that I am a King.   To this end was I born, and for this cause came I into the world."   Mark, dear reader, what for ?   He does not say, to save lost sinners, though that would have been true ; neither does He say, to make the Church My own, though that also would have been blessedly true ; but He says, " To bear witness to the *truth* "—the truth of His *Kingship.*   For *this He died.*   " Shall I crucify your King?" was Pilate's last question before he wrote the title, and put it on the cross : " Jesus of Nazareth, the King of the Jews."

There is yet a fourth aspect of His precious death : Jesus GAVE HIMSELF at the cross as the Man of God's delight, fashioned in God's image, and after His likeness (see Genesis i. 26), Who should by His death redeem *creation* from the bondage of corruption, and bring it into the liberty of the glory of the children of God—that, as " the last Adam," He might possess and have dominion over it eternally for God. Hence the 8th Psalm, and the quotation of it in Hebrews ii.: "Made a little lower than the angels for *the suffering of death,*" that He might be crowned with glory and honour, and might have "*all things* under His feet."

This is, indeed, a wide and glorious aspect of "the sufferings of Christ;" yet a needful one, both for God's glory, that "God may be all in all," and needful also for the fulfilment of God's promise of "new heavens and a new earth, wherein dwelleth righteousness" (2 Peter iii. 13).

But each of these four aspects of Jesus' death was denied and derided at the cross by blinded, guilty man, led on by Satan.

Man and Satan denied at that cross that Jesus died on it as the Substitute FOR the individual sinner; for they placed Him there *between* thieves, thus "numbering Him with the transgressors," as *one of them;* and in this company, and thus placed between them, He remained and died.

Again, man and Satan denied at that cross that it was in *willingness of love* He died; for they bound Him with cords in the garden, as if Jesus would have escaped if He could; and they *nailed* Him to the tree, as though their compulsion could keep Him there, telling Him to come down from the cross if He were *able,* and under this seeming compulsion, Jesus meekly remained and died.

His being *a King*, born such—God's King by birth—was equally there derided. The "crown of thorns" upon His head, was man's expression of this; and, for aught we know, with this mocking of His Kingship still on His blessed brow, He hung upon the cross, and breathed His last. Man's selfishness took off from Him "the scarlet robe" —too valuable, in their eyes, for Him to die in; but we are not told that they relieved Him of the crown of thorns.

And lastly, they equally denied that He was the Man of God's delight. "Let royal apparel be brought for the *man* whom the king *delighteth* to honour," was Haman's word (Esther vi. 7, 8); but the Man of God's delight—His Son, in Whom He was "well pleased"—was not even allowed His own raiment in which to die; and in this nakedness Jesus remained and died.

But there were "glories" to follow; not one of the virtues of His precious death but must be manifested, and every claim of His cross must be vindicated; but where? and how? Not here below, where it is still "man's day," and the time of the "power of darkness." Not by the wisdom, the power, or the religion of the world, which, in the three languages of the then world—the Greek, the Latin, and the Hebrew—were all seen in written mockery over His head, and are all of them against Him still. God is Himself the proclaimer of the excellencies of Christ's death, and the vindicator

of His claim to all for which He there " GAVE
HIMSELF;" and this is seen in God's raising Him
from the dead, and exalting Him to His own right
hand.

First.   In resurrection-glory Jesus is seen as
having been that sinless *Substitute* for the sinner,
which, at His cross, man denied He was.   The
Raised-up One, says Peter (Acts x. 40-43), is shown
openly as the One through Whose " name whosoever believeth in Him shall receive remission of
sins."   "In *Him* all that believe are justified "
(Acts xiii. 39).   And no sooner is He risen, than
sinners by thousands thus look on Him, each one
claiming Him, through faith, and saying with Paul,
" Who loved ME, and gave Himself for ME."

Again.   No sooner is He raised from the dead,
than God gives Him that *Church* which He had
loved, and for which He died.   He comes down
again from heaven to the disciples, in John xx., as
its foundation-stone ; and in Acts ii., in the three
thousand joined to the fellowship of the apostles,
we see the edifice rising into view in this very
world which had so lately denied Him as the
lover of it ; and it still increases, spite of all " the
gates of hell " against it.

Nor is His Kingship any longer obscured ; the
place He occupies as the Risen One makes it plain.
God said to Him, " Sit Thou at My right hand,
till I make Thy foes Thy footstool;" and the
coming kingdom is as fully asserted as belonging

to Jesus as through Him the forgiveness of sinners
is proclaimed, or His love to the Church, and His
lordship over it, is taught.   Paul has no sooner
said, in 1 Timothy i. 15 : " Christ Jesus came into
the world to save sinners," than he adds (verse 17):
" Now unto the KING eternal, immortal, invisible,
the only wise God, be honour and glory for ever
and ever.   Amen."

And God in resurrection has also *clothed* Him,
Whom man, alas! in blindness and wickedness,
hung *naked* on the cross, and left Him thus to die.
God has clothed Him gloriously ; yes, clothed and
crowned Him.   Not yet with the "*many diadems*"
of His reigning day ; they are in reserve for Him
when He comes as " King of kings, and Lord of
lords," and rules this earth for God for a thousand
years.   But God has already " crowned Him with
glory and honour " (Hebrews ii. 9); garlanded Him
($\sigma\tau\epsilon\phi\alpha\nu o\omega$) with the wreath upon His head of the
victory He has won over " that old serpent, which
is the devil," by which victory He has obtained
the earth and heavens for His own, and will replace
them by new heavens and a new earth, which shall
stand for ever.   Yes, Jesus is the Man Whom God
" delighteth to honour," and to Whom dominion
shall ultimately be given over all the works of God.

But all these " glories " are hidden now—hidden
where Christ is hid, in God—where our life is also
hid with Him ; but Christ, Who is our life, shall
appear, and then shall we " also appear with Him

in glory " (Colossians iii. 3, 4); and then will these
glories—fruits of His woes unto death upon the
tree—also, all of them, appear.

At that moment of His glorious appearing, "men
in glory " will be seen with Him—sinners saved—
each of whom He loved, and for each one of whom
He "gave Himself."

Then also will His Church be seen dwelling in
the embrace of His love, the delight of His eyes;
for He has presented her to Himself " glorious,
the Church not having spot, or wrinkle, or any
such thing, but holy and without blemish."

His Kingly throne—"the throne of His own
glory "—will then also have been given Him, and
He will sit upon it, crowned, not with thorns, but
with the glory that will be visibly His, as the "*one*
King over all the earth, and His name *one*"
(Zechariah xiv. 9); while ten thousand thousand
blest ones shall gratefully praise Him, Israel foremost, and the nations also rejoicing to see the
King in His beauty. " Kings shall shut their
mouths at Him : for that which had not been told
them shall they see ; and that which they had not
heard shall they consider " (Isaiah lii. 15).

> " Look, ye saints, the sight is glorious;
> See the 'Man of Sorrows' now,
> From the fight returned victorious;
> Every knee to Him shall bow.
> Crown Him! crown Him!
> Crowns become the Victor's brow."

And lastly. *Creation* will also then begin its
subjection to Jesus as "the last Adam." His

deeds of power over the old and doomed earth and heaven, both of mercy and of judgment, will show this. In the nation of Israel, human life will be again prolonged to an antediluvian length (Isaiah lxv. 20-22); sickness will not be known in Jerusalem, except for sin (Isaiah xxxiii. 24); the very animals will lose their passions in Immanuel's land (Isaiah xi. 6-9); while, on the other hand, the carcases of transgressors shall be visible outside Jerusalem for men's warning, with the worm in them undying, and the fire of their judgment unquenched.

But, better still, the beginning of a "new earth" will then be also seen; for surely the Jerusalem above, the Holy City, ministering "healing to nations" below by the "leaves" of its "tree of life," can be nothing less than a first step toward that entire new earth and new heavens, which, at the close of Jesus' millennial reign, will take the place of the present heavens and earth entirely.

If these things be so, well may Peter speak of the "glories" of Christ that follow His "sufferings." How true, and how variously fulfilled, will be Isaiah's word : " He shall see of the travail of His soul, and shall be satisfied."

In one hour of woe, He bowed His soul, and died, as it were, many "deaths" (Isaiah liii. 9, margin). At the one hour of His glorious appearing, He will be seen possessed of living joys corresponding to all those woes of His death.

Well may our hearts say, " Come, Lord Jesus."

The Miracles at the Cross.

MATTHEW XXVII 45-54.

THE theme that occupies the souls of millions of saved sinners is expressed in the familiar words—

> "When I *survey* the wondrous cross
> On which the King of glory died."

And millions more will yet behold that Holy Sufferer with adoring wonder. But others have looked upon Him, and more will yet look, with very different eyes. " And sitting down, they *watched* Him there," is what is said of the throng of the crucifiers on the hill of Calvary. Yes, they "watched Him;" but it was with the idle, malicious eyes of lovers of sin and haters of God. And what millions, before whom He has been "lifted up," have since looked on Him with similar eyes! By means of the doctrine of Christ, professors of His name have in all ages given passing glances at the cross, and at Him hanging on it; but, alas! neither to trust Him nor to love Him. The cross of Christ has been used simply as a subject for the painted canvas, or as a theme for the mere sounds of music; or, worse still, as a pathetic part of the so-called "Christian religion," by which to dominate over the feelings and conscience of listeners, and by which to enhance priestly power and priestly wealth. But let us dwell on what is happier.

It is not so much to our Lord *Himself* upon the cross, or to the *moral* miracles of righteousness, mercy and love, which faith sees in Him in His dying hour, that we would now turn, but rather to those external miracles which accompanied His wondrous death. These seem to be given us, as *fingers* from God, pointing all beholders to the infinite value of that holy Offering which caused the rending asunder of the Son of God Himself—soul from body—when He died for sin.

Crucifixion was fearfully common in Palestine under Roman rule, and the outward and visible part of the dying of our Lord was simply the yielding up His breath, as any other dying one does. The expression in Matt. xxvii. 50, "yielded up the ghost," is only old English for "gave up His spirit," and does not in the least imply any hastening of His own death by an act of His Divine power. As His blessed head was bowed at that moment, any one of the idle beholders might have said to another, "Ah, the Nazarene is dead!" just as the soldier also saw He was dead before he pierced His side.

But though in appearance like any other dying,

how infinitely different was it in its nature, and character, and value! Hence the need of testimony to its deep and hidden worth. And surely, one part of God's outward testimony to the unparalleled preciousness of the death of His Son, is to be found in the recorded *miracles* that accompanied His dying hour.

The signs and wonders in Egypt compelled even the magicians to say, " This is the finger of God;" and well might the signs and wonders at Calvary extort from all who know of them the centurion's cry, " Truly, this was the Son of God!" But, alas! they do not.

In Matthew's Gospel the miracles recorded are three in number.

1st. The three hours' darkness.

2nd. The rending of the veil of the temple.

3rd. The earthquake by which the graves of sleeping "saints" were opened.

All these could be the finger of God only. They were no part of our Lord's *living* obedience, as were the miracles of feeding the multitudes or the raising of Lazarus from the dead ; nor were they any part of His dying obedience, for He had already breathed His last. They, therefore, contribute nothing to that glorious robe of righteousness which Jesus now is before God for the sinner. Had neither of the three miracles taken place, Christ's perfection for us before God would have been the same. Nor is either of them predicted in Scripture, as were even minute details of the cross, such as the piercing of His blessed side.

What, then, was the object of these miracles? Were they not amongst the outward and visible *tokens* of the unspeakable value of Christ's most precious death? They do not constitute its preciousness, but they direct our attention to what that preciousness really was. They are helps to the sinner's faith in Him. They are solemn waymarks, pointing to the sin-bearing Lamb, of God's providing.

Thus considered, they strengthen our faith, while they also condemn all unbelief. In this the three are alike, but in character of testimony to Christ's death they differ, and also in sphere of application.

(1) The three hours' darkness was for the *whole land;* (2) the rent veil would be for the *priests* in their deeper sinfulness and malice; for only priests, it may be presumed, witnessed its rending; and (3) the opened graves (for three days) of " saints " would be for the *" little flock,"* who had continued with the Lord in His temptations.

But the lessons taught by these three miracles also differ, and on this we may a little enlarge.

(1) The three hours' darkness may serve to remind us of that passing " from darkness to light," which is God's *first* mercy to the sinner by the cross, and the saved sinner's first joy.

(2) The rending of the veil tells us of that unhindered and near "access" to God, to which

believers are called since Christ's death, and which none ever had before.

(3) The opened graves do surely point to that first resurrection of "saints" *only*, at Christ's coming, which is the blessed hope of all who are Christ's. This also was not revealed till the great Head of the Church had died.

The lessons taught by these miracles, it may be observed, embrace the whole earthly course of the believer. (1) Through Christ's death, he passed in one brief moment from darkness into God's marvellous light (see 1 Peter ii. 9); (2) thenceforth during *all* his happy days on earth, he is a worshipper, drawing near to God without a veil between ; and (3) his link with earth *ends* at the moment of "the first resurrection," when he rises in fellowship with Christ's resurrection. How brief the first and last of these trophies of Christ's precious death ; how life-long and precious is that which we are taught by the "rent veil!"

But these events at the "wondrous cross" will reward a closer scrutiny ; for they were stupendous miracles indeed.

"Now from the sixth hour there was darkness over all the land to the ninth hour." Three hours of darkness, from noon to three p.m., the brightest part of the day, and under the blaze of an eastern sun! What hand but God's could give it ? The same Hand that ages before had brought a three-day darkness on less guilty Egypt, now brings a

similarly awful darkness on far guiltier Palestine;
for Abraham's nation was worse than Gentile
Pilate, or his soldiers. Surely, in both instances
it was a God-given warning of the doom and the
darkness of an eternal hell; and it was thus an
arresting mercy from God, to fright them from it.
It was as a writing on "the plaister of the wall,"
in the midst of their godless merry-making over
their Victim's death!

Israel's sins are spoken of as a "*cloud*," and
their transgressions as a "*thick cloud;*" and truly
thick and dark must have been the cloud that
covered Palestine for those three hours, summoned
there by Him Whom darkness obeys, as also does
the light. Alas! it was a too correct emblem of
the nation's iniquities! But all was in vain. Israel
no more repented at this awful miracle than Egypt
or its monarch had done ages before, for—

> " Legal terrors only harden,
> All the while they work alone."

But we are told of the *end* of this darkness, as well
as its coming on. It ceased outwardly at the very
hour when Christ's awful cry told that all the
doom and darkness, due to sinners, had filled His
mighty, suffering soul, and had come between Him
and God. "About the *ninth hour* Jesus cried,
Eli, Eli, lama sabachthani?" When the three
hours' outward emblem of the sinner's dark doom
ceased, the awful and infinite *reality of God's
wrath* was felt in Jesus' own soul. The darkness

which externally ceased, gathered itself up within
the Sufferer's soul. " When Thou shalt make His
SOUL an offering for sin " (Isaiah liii. 10). " Thou
hast laid me in the lowest pit, in DARKNESS, in the
deeps " (Psalm lxxxviii. 8). Yet neither the darkness, while it lasted, nor its sudden ceasing, seems
to have wrought any softening in the bystanders ;
their last act was to mock Him with " vinegar "
to drink. But to us, who do at all

"Survey that wondrous cross,"

how blessed it is to know that Jesus, our Lord
Himself, passed from His soul's deep darkness to
God's own " marvellous light ; " and we also have,
in HIM. In resurrection, God's smile and the light
of His countenance ended for ever to Jesus that
awful darkness ; and now He is to us " the *Light*
of Life."

But the second miracle of the cross, the rending
of the veil of the temple, has its precious teaching
also. The temple being at the south-east extremity
of Jerusalem, was far distant from the hill of
Calvary on the west of the city ; but no sooner did
death rend the Lamb of God, than God rent the
ancient veil from top to bottom, spite of its enclosure
within thick temple walls, and its top being out of
man's reach (some thirty feet high), and its being
woven of the strongest materials. This took place
also at the ninth hour of the day, which seems to
have been a very public hour at the temple (Acts
iii. 1), and many priests would be there. All this

was surely God's testimony to *them;* but their subsequent lies at the tomb of Jesus, too plainly show how they slighted this marvellous event ; and painfully suggest how boldly they would dare to sew up the veil again !

But to us the veil is now *for ever rent;* and we who were born into light out of darkness by a "look at the Crucified One," are now worshippers in the light of the unveiled presence of God and the Lamb. No "rood-screen" now intervenes ; *all believers* are equally saints and priests, and equally brought within the veil by Jesus' death.

These are the New Testament gifts of God to us, and we should sin against God if we denied them ; nor should we ignore them by sanctioning with our presence a worship that sets them aside. The moment we do so, we begin to bring a *veil over our spirits*, and put ourselves back, more or less, into the place of Old Testament worshippers. But it was to deliver His saints from all "veiled" and distant worship, that Jesus died.

The third miracle recorded in Matthew is that of an earthquake, which occurred at the same mighty moment, an earthquake so violent, that by it the "rocks rent" (Palestine being a most rocky soil), and yet so God-guided was it, that it simply opened the graves of sleeping saints, leaving others' graves untouched. After three days the sleepers awoke when Christ arose, and they entered the "holy city and appeared to many."

c

To faith, the graves of sleeping saints now lie open, so to speak, and the brief "three days'" interval will soon pass, so near is the coming of our Lord; and then, while the rest of the dead continue in their graves, these sleepers will awake, and will enter the "holy city," the "holy Jerusalem," of Revelation xxi. 10, and appear (shine forth) to many; for, "when Christ, Who is our life, shall appear, then shall ye also appear with Him in glory" (Colossians iii. 4).

God's Edens.

Gen ii 8, xlix. 20, Psalm xxxvi. 8; Prov. xxix. 17.

THE word "*Eden*" means "delight," or "pleasure," and in the Hebrew it is used in all the above passages. From them we learn the different Edens in which God Himself either has had pleasure, or now has pleasure, or yet will have.

God once had *pleasure* in the garden in which He put our first parents, for He planted it eastward in "Eden"—the place of "delight;" and Genesis ii. 8-14, shows us what it must have been. God Himself could rest in it! He beheld it, and it was "very good" (Genesis i. 31).

But sin defiled, and therefore ruined it. *That* "Eden," *that* delight of the eyes and heart of God, has passed away, never to be recalled; the very spot where it was, cannot be found. God no longer takes "delight" in this creation; it yields Him no "Eden." Dear child of God, remember this, and deeply ponder it, to help you against making earthly things in any degree *your* "pleasure" or "delight."

But Genesis xlix. 20, points us to " Edens " yet
to come. Dying Jacob is declaring things that
shall be true of his sons " in *the last days*," and
says, " Out of Asher his bread shall be fat, and he
shall yield royal *dainties;*" *i.e.*, " royal delights "
or " kingly Edens;" for the word in the Hebrew
is the same.

Are we not thus reminded that, as He did at the
first, so " the God of Jacob," the " God of all
grace," will, ere long, yet bless Israel, and make
to Himself out of that nation " pleasures " and
" delights," even in a world in which His former
" delight " in His creation-work is all blighted and
gone ?

But in Psalm xxxvi. 8, this happy word comes
again, as if to tell us that even NOW, before the
day of Asher's and Israel's *future* " kingly Edens,"
the tried Psalmist tastes the Eden-like pleasures
of God's love to him. True, " the transgression
of the wicked" is before his view, and fills his
heart with pain; but from verse 5 onward, the
glorious grace of his God so *fills* his view that he
cries out, " How excellent is Thy loving-kindness,
O God! therefore the children of men put their
trust under the shadow of Thy wings. They shall
be abundantly satisfied with the fatness of Thy
house; and Thou shalt make them drink of the
river of Thy pleasures;" *i.e.*, " Thy *Edens.*"

As if David would say, Our father Jacob's dying
prophecy is not fulfilled yet; Asher does not yet

yield "royal Edens;" but my faith, and the faith of all "servants of the Lord" (see title, Psalm xxxvi.), *does* drink of the river of God's Edens even now! And mark, it is "*Edens.*" Creation, at its first and best, had but a *single* Eden; but when "grace triumphant reigns," it shall make *many* "Edens" for both God and man in the restored and blest Israel nation; and even NOW, before that day comes, the souls of patient saints and "servants of the Lord" do drink of the river of God's many "Edens," in spite of all the scene around them of sin and sorrow.

But Proverbs xxix. 17, shows, perhaps, a deeper lesson still. "Correct thy son," says Solomon, "and he shall give thee rest; yea, he shall give *delight* ("delights," "Edens;" see Hebrew) unto thy soul."

And if this be God's law for human family life, is it not also His own way of getting to Himself "Edens" of pleasure and delight from *us* as HIS children?

What says Paul in Hebrews xii. 9-11? "We have had fathers of our flesh which corrected us, and we gave them reverence: shall we not much rather be in subjection unto the Father of spirits, and live? For they verily for a few days chastened us after their own pleasure; but He for our profit, that we might *be partakers of His holiness.* Now no chastening for the present seemeth to be joyous, but grievous: nevertheless, afterward it yieldeth

the peaceable fruit of righteousness unto them which
are *exercised* thereby."

Yes, beloved fellow-saints, let us welcome God
our Father's corrections, that we may give HIM
"rest;" yea, that we may give HIM gardens of
delight, and Edens to HIS soul.

Job gave God these "delights" when he *fully*
bowed to the correction laid on him, and said (Job
xlii. 2), "I know Thou canst do everything, and
that no thought of Thine can be hindered . . .
Wherefore I abhor myself, and repent in dust and
ashes."

David's heart yielded to God these "Edens" of
delight when he said (Psalm li. 12), "Restore unto
me the joy of Thy salvation, and uphold me with
Thy free Spirit."

So, too, Hezekiah, when submitting to God's
correction, said, "O Lord, by these things men
live, and in all these things is the life of my spirit"
(Isaiah xxxviii. 16).

And richly did Paul yield the same when he
bowed to the correction and discipline of the
"thorn in the flesh," and said, "Most gladly
therefore will I rather glory in my infirmities,
that the power of Christ may rest upon me" (see
2 Corinthians xii. 9).

How blessed, then, is this! There is not a child
of God anywhere who is under his God and
Father's correcting hand, and is duly "exercised
thereby," who does not yield to God's heart, even

now, "Edens" of delight such as all creation cannot yield, and could not even at its former best estate; and such as Jacob's nation cannot give Him until the day when "IT also shall turn to the Lord," and "ALL Israel shall be saved."

Cheer up, then, tried child of God, and ask for the north wind and the south wind alike to blow upon your garden, that the spices of it may flow out, in order that your Beloved may come into His garden, and may eat His pleasant fruits (see Solomon's Song iv. 16); and no sooner do you truly say it than the next verse (v. 1) shows you what an "Eden" of delights He has found in your love to Him; for He says, "I am come into My garden, My sister, My spouse: I have gathered My myrrh with My spice; I have eaten My honeycomb with My honey; I have drunk My wine with My milk: eat, O friends; drink, yea, drink abundantly, O beloved [ones]."

God's Shadows.

"Safe in the arms of Jesus,
  Safe on His gentle breast;
There, by His love *o'ershaded*,
  Sweetly my soul shall rest."

SO runs one of the hymns often sung amongst us, that has edified and cheered many; and as we have just seen that God has "Edens" of delight for us in His Word, so has He *shadows* for us of protection and blessing with which His love overshadows us; for there is not an object in creation around us, nor a season of the year, nor an event of our lives, and especially not a want, nor a woe, by which He would not instruct us, and draw us nearer to Himself. And the time of the year has now come when even in this temperate climate a *shadow* from the heat is welcome, and to some absolutely necessary. Let us profit by this summer heat; and as we seek the shady side of the crowded street, or the cooling shadow of the seaside rock, or of the leafy trees, let us call to mind the emblem God has made *shadows* to be of His great salvation.

Let us remember, then, first, The shadow of the *cloud* over Israel in the desert (Exodus xiii. 20-22;

Psalm cv. 38, 39); second, The shadow of the
rock (Isaiah xxxii. 2); third, The shadow of the
wings (Psalm lxiii. 7); and fourth, The shadow
of the *Bridegroom's love* (Solomon's Song ii. 3).

The first of these may be called, The shadow of
deliverance; the second, The shadow of ever-flow-
ing supply; the third, The shadow of loving protection; and the fourth, The shadow of rejoicing
love. Well may we say, "Oh, the blessings of
him whose transgression is forgiven, and whose sin
is covered!" (Psalm xxxii. i. See Hebrew.)

1. The *shadowing cloud* over the camp of Israel
presents a wonderful object for our instruction.
Without it, in the burning heat of an Arabian
desert, that vast multitude must have perished.
Their supposed number of three millions must
have covered, when encamped, some twelve square
miles of ground! In their tents were the aged, and
also the feeble infants. How absolutely necessary
to them the shelter of that cloud! as needful, one
would think, as the very water they drank. And
God raised it over them, and kept it there; for
while we are told in Exodus xiii. that it was in the
form of a " pillar " that guided them, Psalm cv. 39
tells us that " He spread a cloud for a *covering*."
What an emblem of the sinner's need of a God-
provided shelter from the burning wrath of God!
What an emblem, too, was that abiding cloud of
Him whom God has " exalted with His right hand
a Prince and a Saviour, to give repentance to

Israel, and remission of sins" (Acts v. 31), under
Whose shelter none can perish!

The " pillar of the cloud," which, as it were, bore
up this welcome shade above them, stood at the
tabernacle door—that tabernacle into which the
blood of the sacrifice had been carried; and the
cloud of God's saving care of them was thus one
expression to them, among many, of His acceptance of the blood of the morning and evening lamb.
And what joy to us now is Christ's shade over us
of His abiding power as a Saviour, since His
being thus exalted is the fruit of God's perfect rest
in His one offering—His one redemption of us by
His blood! for in Him " we have redemption
through His blood, even the forgiveness of sins,"
and are thus " blessed with all spiritual blessing in
the heavenly places " in Him.　No lapse of time,
no burning sun of the desert, could remove that
cloud, or deprive the Israelites of its wonderful
protection; for it was given them by God, and He
established it; and does not Christ " save *to the
uttermost* them that come to God by Him?"

2. But there is the *shadow of the rock*, as well as
that of the cloud.　Shelter from the burning heat
is in this shadow, as well as in the former; but
there is also shelter from the *storm* and from the
tempest.　It is an emblem to us of Christ as *King*,
as well as Saviour.　See Isaiah xxxii. 1, 2: " Behold, a *King* shall reign in righteousness　.　.　.
And a *Man* shall be as an hiding-place from the

wind, and a covert from the tempest; . . . as
the shadow of a great *rock* in a weary land."

A rock will not give way when the wind is
carrying all else before it, and the tempest beats.
Such the dying thief found Christ to be—a Saviour
King; and, sheltering at His side, the storm and
tempest of hell-deserving doom could not reach
him. Nay, more, much more, the "great Rock"
was not only his shelter from the "horrible tempest" (see Psalm xi. 6) which God must "rain upon
the wicked," but he was speedily hidden in the
cleft of that Rock, and was that very day in
Paradise along with his Saviour-King, as a pledge
of being with Him when He comes in His kingdom. Such also Saul of Tarsus found Christ to
be. The voice to him from heaven on the
Damascus road, might justly have been "hailstones
and coals of fire"—"an horrible tempest;" but he
sheltered beneath the mighty One as a "great
rock," and "obtained mercy" (see 1 Timothy i. 13),
and ever after delighted to say, " Now unto *the
King* eternal, immortal, invisible, the only wise
God, be honour and glory for ever and ever.
Amen" (1 Timothy i. 17).

But in the shadow of the rock is *supply*, as well
as deliverance; for deliverance is not enough;
there *must* also be supply. Noah, delivered from
the flood, needed to have all food in the ark; and
Israel, shaded by the cloud, or by the shadow of
the rock, still needed constant supply; as Elijah

did also when hidden by God from wicked Ahab: and from the rock the supply came. And, oh, what glory to God at each step of that supply! It was as contrary to nature as it was that the sheltering cloud should continue in spite of the burning heat. Water from a *dry* rock! Wonderful, yet true! "Tremble, thou earth, at the presence of the Lord (Hebrew, Adon, *i.e.*, King), at the presence of the God of Jacob; Which turned the rock into a standing water, the flint into a fountain of waters" (Psalm cxiv. 7, 8). And we know *how* it was, by God's standing on it in Horeb, and its being smitten (Exodus xvii. 6).

And thus is Christ our *supply*, as well as our shelter. Nor of water only; the rock gave honey also, and even oil. So Moses reminds Israel: "The Lord alone did lead him . . . And He made him to suck *honey* out of the rock, and oil out of the flinty rock" (Deuteronomy xxxii. 12, 13). Wondrous streams truly, from such a source! But God "is able;" and Paul tells us "that rock was Christ." No wonder, then, that God made it such as never any rock was before. Only then could it at all set forth the fulness of supply there is in Christ for us, and then but feebly. Those who pass through "the valley of Baca," with Christ as their rock, not only "make it a well," but also sing, "The Lord God is a sun and shield: He will give grace and glory: *no good thing* will He withhold from them that walk uprightly. O

Lord of hosts, blessed is the man that trusteth in Thee " (Psalm lxxxiv. 11, 12).

But God provided also "a clift" in the rock, that Moses, being put there by God, and covered with His hand, might behold His glory (Exodus xxxiii. 22). Moses longed to behold it, as John in Patmos wept to have the book opened (Rev. v.). " I beseech thee, show me Thy glory," was Moses' prayer ; and though it was but in part, only God's " back parts," and not His " face," yet Moses needed to be strengthened in the *clift of the rock*, and covered with God's hand, in order to bear it. But God's rock supplied this need also ; and Moses by it anticipated, in some measure, our New Testament days of unveiled things, and, like John in Patmos, heard and learned what others did not. Water, honey, oil, and the strengthening clift for knowing more of God, are rich lessons to us of Christ as our Rock of supply, as well as shadow.

3. But there is also the *shadow of the wings.* This tells of tenderest affection. The parent bird uses all the strength and softness of its wings for the protection and fostering and growth of its brood. Thus hidden, the hawk does not even see them ; and they are cherished and kept sensible of their parent's affection. How blessed that God should use such an emblem of His heart and ways of love to us ! Old Testament and New both use it. " He shall cover thee with His feathers, and

under His *wings* shalt thou trust," says the Psalmist (probably Moses), in Psalm xci. 4. " Hide me under the shadow of Thy *wings*," says David (Psalm xvii. 8) ; and again, when " in the wilderness of Judah," " Because Thou hast been my help, therefore in the shadow of Thy *wings* will I rejoice" (Psalm lxiii. 7). And when the Lord Jesus would express His yearning, but rejected, love for Jerusalem, He says, " How often would I have gathered thy children together, even as a hen gathereth her chickens under her *wings*, and ye would not !" (Matthew xxiii. 37.)

The shadow of the *wings* seems especially for times and circumstances of sorrow and trial. Moses (as we suppose) gives assurance of it in Psalm xci., when the arrow was flying by day, and the terror by night ; David, in Psalm xvii., when the wicked were oppressing him ; and in Psalm lxiii., when he fain would have gone to the sanctuary if he could, but his enemies were "seeking his soul to destroy it." And when is parental affection and overshadowing care so sweet as then ? Wayworn Moses and persecuted David could appeal to it ; and so may all such now. Ruth also had it stretched over her in the heat and toil of all her long gleaning through " barley harvest and wheat harvest." No wonder she did not leave the field of Boaz for any other, since it was *his* lips had said to her, " The Lord recompense thy work, and a full reward be given thee of the Lord God of Israel, *under Whose wings* thou ait come to trust" (Ruth ii. 12). Oh, may *workers*, then, as well as *sufferers*, abide under the shadow of the *wings* of the Almighty! and this they will surely do, if they dwell "in the *secret place*" of His love to them in Christ (see Psalm xci. 1).

4. But there is a fourth overshadowing of God's favour to us, yet richer than these. It is the *shadow of the Bridegroom's rejoicing love.* "I sat down under His *shadow*," says the bride in Solomon's Song ii. 3, "with great delight, and His fruit was sweet to my taste." The scene shown us here is one of no fear, and no care. It is the repose of undisturbed enjoyment, though in a world of sin and sorrow, and with danger not far away. The "daughters of Jerusalem," the ensnaring things of "the city" and its "streets and broadways," are near—too near; but she is in His "house of wine," "His banner over her is love," and as long as she is delighting in "His shadow" over her, and finds sweet fruit in His love to her, as well as shade, He charges none to molest her. This richest, sweetest shade of all is, therefore, our life-long proper portion, and can only be lost as we ourselves surrender it. Compare John xiv. 23: "Jesus answered and said unto him, If a man love Me, he will keep My words: and My Father will love him, and We will come unto him, and make Our ABODE with him."

Nothing here below can excel this overshadowing

love of the Bridegroom over the bride. Well
may we once more say—

> " There, by His love o'ershaded,
>   Sweetly my soul shall rest."

But what next ?

> " Hark ! 'tis the voice of angels,
>   Borne in a song to me,
>   Over the fields of glory,
>   Over the jasper sea."

Yes, the best that even His love *can* give us here
below, only points us to the fulness ere long at
Jesus' speedy and blessed coming again. The
home of glory will itself be an overshadowing.
The transfiguration scene was given to Christ for
us as a specimen of " the power and coming of our
Lord Jesus Christ," and there we are told (Matt.
xvii. 5) of the glorified ones, that " a bright cloud
overshadowed them ;" not indeed for protection, for
danger and sorrow come not there, but as an
answer to Peter's ardent wish to make the passing
glory permanent, and to build tabernacles. No
wonder it says that the favoured three in mortal
bodies " feared as *they* (*i.e.*, the glorified ones)
entered the cloud." Heavenly things overwhelm
our poor mortal faculties, but God reveals them
even now to faith ; and Peter makes good use in
his second epistle of having been an eye-witness of
the majesty of our Lord.

John also saw the countless multitude who had
come out of the great tribulation, and the Lamb so

dwelling "*over* them" (see Greek, Rev. vii. 15), "that they would neither hunger nor thirst any more; nor the sun light on them, nor any heat."

Yes, that is God's final and everlasting overshadowing of us. And if it is said of Jerusalem and Zion below, during the thousand years' reign, that God "will rejoice *over* her with joy, will rest (Hebrew, be silent) in His love, and will joy *over* her with singing" (see Zephaniah iii. 17), how much more will He overshadow with the brightness of His infinite delight ALL the glorified redeemed in His eternal new creation? In glad anticipation we can sing—

> " Joyful now the new creation
> Rests in undisturbed repose ;
> Blessed in Jesus' full salvation,
> Sorrow now nor thraldom knows.

> " Hark ! the heavenly notes again !
> Louder swells the song of praise !
> Throughout creation's vault, Amen !
> Amen, responsive joy doth raise."

But there are *shadows to be warned of*, as well as God's shadows to be delighted in.

" Woe to the rebellious children, saith the Lord, that take counsel, but not of Me ; and that cover with a covering, but not of My Spirit, that they may add sin to sin: that walk to go down into Egypt, and have not asked at My mouth; to strengthen themselves in the strength of Pharaoh, and to trust in the *shadow of Egypt !*" (Isaiah xxx. 1, 2.)

D

Wealth, and worldly wisdom, and human army-power, are not these the shadow of Egypt now, as they were in Isaiah's days? Only now with more self-confidence and arrogance, and with hearts more hardened because of more of God's love re-sisted, and with a deeper darkness because of greater light sinned against. " I sit as a queen, and am no widow, and shall see no sorrow," is Babylon's language up to her very hour of over-throw, and tells of how completely " the shadow of Egypt " is her trust ; but " when they shall say, Peace and safety, then sudden destruction cometh upon them, as travail upon a woman with child ; and they shall not escape " (1 Thessalonians v. 3). No wonder He says, " Come out of her, my people."

Nor must we, like Jonah, make for ourselves even the *shadow of a booth*. This is a special temptation to God's servants " who labour in word and doctrine." Jonah wearied at the long-suffering of God's ways with the wicked, as Job did with the length of God's afflictions on him. But whether in suffering or in service, we must " let patience have her *perfect work*," if we would be " perfect and entire, lacking nothing." No sooner do we cease fellowship with God's pity toward an unsaved " Nineveh-world," than, like Demas, we love " this present world," and make for ourselves some booth under which to sit and selfishly watch the scene.

Once more God had a shadow at hand ; but this time it was one of mighty, yet gentle, reproof. In a night a gourd grew sufficiently to give Jonah its shade ; but *only for that day :* it withered the next morning, but left for Jonah a lasting lesson. May we so truly learn it as one amongst the many things " written aforetime for our learning," that we may all our days abide in Christ, whether in service or in suffering, and sit under no shadow but that of His love, even till the day of His coming and His kingdom. Amen.

God's Mighty Moments.

ONE of the "words of the wise" which we sometimes see on the walls of fellow-believers' houses, is as follows :—

"LOST,

SOMEWHERE BETWEEN SUNRISE AND SUNSET,

TWO GOLDEN HOURS,

EACH SET WITH SIXTY DIAMOND MINUTES.

NO REWARD IS OFFERED,

AS THEY ARE

LOST FOR EVER!"

" Two golden hours " is more, we would trust, than any of our readers ever do lose between any " sunrise and sunset " of their precious ransomed time (though we little know, perhaps, any of us, how much we lose) ; yet the motto on a wall may help us to " watch and pray," and may stir us to be diligent in catching the moments as they come, and in using them for God's glory as they fly past.

Paul writes to us about " redeeming the time " (Ephesians v. 16) in the same epistle in which he tells of the love that chose us in Christ " before the foundation of the world," and that also reaches on to the "ages to come;" and in his epistle to the Romans, though dwelling so largely on "the gospel of God" (Romans i. 1), "the everlasting God" (Romans xvi. 26), he yet also says, "Knowing the time, that now it is high time to awake out of sleep : . . . . the night is far spent, the day is at hand" (Romans xiii. 11, 12).

Peter also makes the same use of the flight of time : " But the end of all things is at hand : be ye *therefore* sober, and watch unto prayer " (1 Peter iv. 7).

Even the heathen philosophers could teach that the only way of taking hold of time was as it approached, and drew the figure of one hasting on, with a lock of hair on his forehead by which you might grasp him ; but no such lock behind, if once you let him pass.

We sing of "God's mighty moments" in our hymns, and we well may.

> " O God, what cords of love are Thine !
>   How gentle, yet how strong !
> Thy truth and grace their power combine
>   To draw our souls along.
>
> " The guilt of twice ten thousand sins
>   ONE MOMENT takes away ;
> And when the fight of faith begins,
>   Our strength is as our day."

And again—

> "Each *moment* listening for the voice,
>   ' Rise up, and come away.' "

Cowper justly says of the creation wonders of

the living God, as shown by the microscope, "To Whom an *atom* is an ample world." And of the God of grace and salvation, we may as truly say, To Him a *moment* is an ample time.

A moment is, strictly speaking, time so short that it could not be made shorter, and is represented by the quickest possible action of the body—"the twinkling of an eye;"* or a moment is but a *point* (see Luke iv. 5: Greek), a thing too small to have in it any size that can be measured. And yet in but a MOMENT, what cannot the God of our salvation do!

We would name three of "God's mighty moments" of blessing to His saved ones :—

1. The moment of conversion.

2. The moment of departing and being with Christ.

3. The moment of the first resurrection.

Each of these wonders of His grace and power is the work of but a *moment*, showing in this respect the glory of God, and in this way meeting also our utmost need.

First, then, our actual passing "from death unto life"—our conversion—was a thing of but a moment. It was by a life-look we were saved, as by a life-look the bitten and dying Israelites were healed, and as by a beam of the glory of the risen Lord Jesus, Saul was brought to God on the

---

* " In a moment," says Paul (1 Corinthians xv. 52), " in the twinkling of an eye ; " an atom being a thing so cut and subdivided that it cannot be subdivided any more.

Damascus road. And nothing short of this could fully manifest God's glory in the sinner's salvation, nor fully meet the dying sinner's need. In the first creation God had but to say, " Let there be light," and light entered amidst the darkness ; and with equal instantaneousness does He shine "in our hearts, to give the light of the knowledge of His glory in the face of Jesus Christ " (2 Cor. iv. 6).

The passing from death unto life may not always seem to be a thing of a moment ; there seems in some cases, both to quickened ones themselves and to those who look on, a longer time and a slower process, but all this is either the struggle of un-belief, previous to the moment of life-giving faith in Christ, or else the action and growth of the new-born life after its springing into being, and must be distinguished in our thoughts from "the time of love " (Ezekiel xvi. 8), the moment of mercy, when the God of salvation " passed by," saw us in our blood, and said unto us, " Live." That was the first to us of " God's mighty moments " for our eternal blessing.

What joy it is to remember this in our gospel work with the still unsaved, that *even* the *moment* of some word to them by your lips, dear reader, is time enough for God to make them his own *for ever ;* and nothing else could suit the case of dying hearers, " whose breath is (only) in their nostrils," and the moment of your voice to them may be the last moment they have. Such was the joy of

Moses in bidding dying Israelites look up to the serpent of brass, and such, too, the glory of God in giving the healing virtue by but a moment's look.

No wonder we sing to the unsaved—

" There is life in a look at the crucified One,
There is life *at this moment* for thee ;
Then look, sinner, look unto Him and be saved —
Unto HIM Who was nailed to the tree."

But the departure of a saved one to be with Christ is another of " God's mighty moments." For the saint to depart is for him to be with Christ in a moment. The Scripture places no interval whatever between the two things. One moment we *live* to the Lord, in dying pain and weakness perhaps, but still living, and living to Him ; the next moment yield up the labouring breath, and die *to Him.* The dying is as truly *to Him* as the living was *to Him*, while still in the body.

And this is another of the triumphs of God's grace to us *through Christ*, and therefore is another of His mighty moments for our blessing. Old Testament saints had not this joy so clearly shown them, nor could they have ; for Christ had not then actually gained the victory which He has now gained by His wondrous death and resurrection. From the hour, yes, the moment of that blessed victory, we date His lordship over the dead as well as the living, of His saints and servants. " For to this end," says the Apostle (Romans xiv. 9), " Christ both died, and revived, *that He might be*

Lord both of the dead and living." Hence the
dying of saints *now* is not a going to the dimness of
Hades, but the entrance in a moment to the joy
of Paradise—the blessedness of being "with
Christ" (compare Luke xxiii. 43, with Phil. i. 23).

Such is the joy of each departing child of God
in this age since the Son of God has come; but
this, like the former one of soul-quickening, is a
moment of God's love and power to His saved
ones *singly and individually*, and precious though
they are, neither of these completes His blessing.
The departed saints are waiting, as we the living
also are, for "the resurrection of the just," and
this will be indeed a crowning one of "God's
mighty moments;" for Paul tells us (1 Cor. xv. 52),
that even this also will be "in a moment, in
the twinkling of an eye, at the last trump: for the
trumpet shall sound, and the dead shall be raised
incorruptible, and we shall be changed." And yet
it shall be but "a moment!" But what a mighty
moment! How glorious, how vast, and yet how
accurate; how perfect and eternally enduring will
be the work that God shall do in that moment!

And if this is true as to the changing of *all* the
living saints at that blessed moment, who shall
one and all be then clothed with bodies glorious,
our wonder still increases as we think of the vast
multitude of those who shall then be lying asleep
in Christ. The earth we live upon and walk upon
has the dust of the human dead mingled in with

its original soil; and mingled in again with both it
and them, lies the ransomed dust of God's saints.
It is *this* He calls for at that mighty moment, and
ALL of it instantly answers to the call (see Job
xiv. 15, xix. 25-27; and 1 Corinthians xv. 38, 42-44);
and that, too, not only from the dry land, but also
from the far larger sea. Forth they come, all of
them with their own dust changed from "corruption" into "incorruption," and from "dishonour"
into "glory;" and that, too, whether buried more
lately or long before, no matter whether gently
laid by loving hands, or beheaded like faithful,
honoured, John the Baptist, or reduced to ashes
like the martyred ones of Smithfield and Madrid,
or of the Church's earlier days. They all, one
generation after another, bore the image of "the
first man"—"earthy;" but now, in one single
moment, they are all "clothed upon," and, behold, they bear "the image of the heavenly!"

Oh! is it not a crowning one of "God's mighty
moments" for our blessing? and that not individually only, but for the "Church glorious"
collectively? How parallel it runs with that other
mighty moment when Christ "loved the Church,
and gave Himself for it!" With *one* mighty stoop,
He bore her sins and her guilt, when God gathered
and laid the burden upon Him; and sinking in
death, He put it all away for ever. At *one* deep
draught, He drained her cup of wrath, when He
tasted death for each one (Hebrews ii. 9); and now,

at *one* mighty moment of triumph, as " the Captain of their salvation," He brings the " many sons unto glory."

Indeed, out of that truly *omnipotent* moment of Jesus' death, flow all these other mighty moments of God's grace and power, which we have been considering ; and not these only, but all the countless multitude of His other moments of " goodness and mercy," which not only so follow us all the days of our life below, but shall flow on for ever in the new creation home of the unveiled presence of God and the Lamb.

" A moment of time is a monument of mercy " is a trite saying around us, but a true one, as respects the unsaved ; but how unspeakably precious are the moments of God's children as they fly ! We would not have them less swift, but we would be stirred by the subject now before us, and by the opening of another year, to value them, and enrich them, as they come and go.

This wondrous grace of God to us in Christ, should now make every moment precious to us between the past one of our conversion and the coming one of our either resting from our labours and being " with Christ," or, better still, our hearing the trump of God, and the shout of the Lord Jesus, and our meeting Him in the air.   But does it ? We sing in our happy Lord's Day assemblies—

" *Sweet the moments*, rich in blessing,
Which before the cross we spend ;'

but might we not have all our other moments of consciousness here below made also sweet to us, if we did but abide in Christ, and His words abode in us? (John xiv. 23.) Shall we excuse henceforth a single moment of our time that we spend away from Christ, and in sloth, or sin, or folly?

Does not the blessed Holy Ghost dwell in us every moment? and does HE not so estimate the mighty moment of Jesus' death for us, and the happy moment when at our believing He first took up His abode in us, that He would not leave us to have from that time forth *one* barren or idle moment during all our time below, even as He knows we shall never have an idle or sinning moment in the blest eternity of our heavenly home?

Oh, then, fellow-saints, let us not grieve the Holy Ghost, Who so graciously ceases not to dwell in us, and never will!

But this will want an unceasing watchfulness on our part; for Satan can make great attacks on us, even in passing moments. It was in but "*a moment of time*" that he made "all the kingdoms of the world," "and the glory of them," pass before our blessed Master (see Luke iv. 5, 6); but no moment of His life-service ever found Him unguarded, or out of the presence of His God, as His instant answer showed: "It is written," said He, "Thou shalt worship the Lord thy God, and Him only shalt thou serve."

Alas! alas! how often it is not so with us!   A

far smaller bait than "all the kingdoms of ·the world" suffices to allure our eye, and even to draw our hearts away for a time from God our Father's love, and Christ our Redeemer's cross, just because we forget the presence with us of our gracious God, and fail to use, as Jesus did, "the sword of the Spirit, which is the Word of God." Thus Peter forgot, on one painful occasion, both the Divine power of his Master and the word of Scripture which his Master's lips had taught him (Matthew xxvi. 31, 32), and in one brief *moment* of a maid-servant's challenge of him, denied the Master Whom he loved! Thus also David, yielding to ease and sloth at the very season "when kings go out to battle," sends Joab with the army, and he tarries at home, and the fatal moment of His glance at Bath-sheba—fatal to his domestic peace ever after —was Satan's moment of darting an arrow into him of unholy lust! (See 2 Samuel xi.)

Yes, fellow-saints, Satan can indeed do us much hurt in but a moment of our sinful unwatchfulness, and can change the moments that should have been as diamonds of heavenly value to us for ever, into wounds which may take long to heal.

The Lord's Supper.

FOR true participation in the Lord's Supper a heavenly conscience is deeply needed, or else the Scriptural frequency with which we partake of it, viz., each first day of the week, will degenerate into a *habit*. It will then simply be a weekly custom, flattering the observers of it with a subtle and hardening sense of self-approval, rather than the holy, happy, yet self-abasing feast that it was meant to be, and which it always is to humble souls.

Observe, first : It is a " SUPPER," and a supper means a substantial and satisfying meal. The very Greek word, used in the New Testament, is derived from one that has reference to the huntsman's hearty meal, which, after toil and fasting, he so relishes. Such should be the Lord's Supper to us spiritually. It should be to our souls a full and satisfying meal, abundant in quantity, and also exactly suited to our taste; as *abundant* as were the seven loaves to the five thousand, which left seven large baskets over; and the food supplied so *appreciated*, that the hungry multitude crossed the sea for more of it. Oh, for a similar hunger, and like esteem for the diet of redeeming love set forth in the Lord's Supper! Indeed, one may say, God never provides either *small* suppers or *unsuited* ones, whether it be the Supper for unsaved sinners in the Gospel, or His Supper for His saints (see Luke xiv. 16, and Revelation iii. 18-20), for He always expects hungry guests, and He fills them "with good things."

It was at the institution of this Supper that our Lord asked for a "guest-chamber," and it is as His *guests* He regards us when we are seated at it. We all know the interest we feel in our guests. At an ordinary human supper, how concerned a kind host is that his guests should sup well, having provided the best his house affords; and he is grieved if he sees that it is slighted, or not relished. How much more does Jesus, our Lord, observe whether our appetite for His Supper is good and keen! And how grieved must He be when His guests are either absent from it altogether, or make use of the heavenly provision in a listless and formal way!

True, it is only ordinary, every-day bread that He puts on the table, and simple, ordinary wine. But in HIS eyes Who provides it, how costly and full of meaning is that bread, and how precious the wine! And verily they should be a rich feast also to our souls. To the believing, hungry soul, they will be so; but to those who are, Laodicea-like, "rich and increased with goods," that is, earthly things, or any form of *self*, what a merely

outward act will be the "breaking of bread," and
what a shell without its true and blessed kernel
will be the entire Supper!

The partaking of the Lord's Supper is so simple,
and occupies so little time, that only true preparation of heart and previous meditation can give
Divine and proper weight, and fulness, to so brief
an act.

The attitude in which we partake of it is also
significant. Our Lord took the Passover reclining
on a couch, and followed it with the breaking of
bread and the cup, and in that same reclining
attitude the disciples received it, and obeyed His
word, "Drink ye all of it." But they knew the
murderous character of Jerusalem, and their
Master's warning, that His death was at hand,
helped to give emphasis to His word, "Do this in
remembrance of Me."

Now, week by week, we sit at the Lord's Table
in comparatively smooth surroundings, and the
holy feast is soon over. Oh, then, how much the
more do we need a Lord's-day morning to prepare
ourselves for it beforehand, and also to watch
against wandering thoughts when the hour for
partaking comes! Prayer, reading, and meditation
on Christ's "wondrous cross," and on God's love
to us in giving Him, are surely the chief means of
obtaining a heavenly appetite for the Lord's Supper.
But how can the idle saint, who, perhaps, has left
his bed later of a Lord's-day morning than other

mornings of the week, or the worldly-minded and sin-excusing saint, who has not judged himself for careless walk and lightsome talk during the week— how can such expect to find in the morsel of bread and the sip of wine which the Lord's Table provides, any real *supper* at all ? No ; God gives His spiritual bread only to the hungry, and of His costly wine of redeeming love He is equally careful (see Proverbs xxxi. 4-7).

One word more. This God-given appetite, of which we speak, is in two forms. There is first the appetite of *conscience*, and then that of *affection*.

As saints who frequent the Lord's Table, we need to have a conscience about all sins and wanderings of which God's good Spirit has made us aware, since the previous occasion we sat as partakers. For how can we learn to live godly in Christ Jesus, except we have, and also cultivate, a tender conscience ? As we look back on the days and hours of the past week, and are reminded of failure and shortcoming, which we have had to confess to our Father and God, how *sweet* and *rich* becomes that broken loaf to us at the Lord's Supper ! Every crumb of it reminds us that Jesus was bruised on the tree for our sins ; yes, for ALL of them ; for HE died for every sin of our believing days, as well as for those of our unregeneracy.

> " His precious blood was shed,
> His body bruised for SIN ;
> REMEMBERING THIS, we break the bread,
> And joyful drink the wine."

E

Or again we sing—

> " Here conscience ends its strife ;
> And faith delights to prove
> The sweetness of the bread of life,
> The fulness of Thy love."

And as the hunger of conscience is satisfied and ends, the sweet and happy hungering and thirsting of *love* only grows within us.   We inwardly long after Him Who has so truly lifted off us "sin's accursed load."

> " Here we forget our griefs and pains;
> We drink, but still our thirst remains:
> Only the Fountain-head above
> Can satisfy the thirst of love."

This is a blessed hunger and a precious thirst, and it shall one day be satisfied (see Matthew v. 6). Hence it is that hungering and thirsting saints would fain prolong the Lord's Supper, instead of stinting either its frequency or its length, did other service to Christ but allow of it.   Hence, too, the precious frequency with which the Pentecost saints kept it (see Acts ii. 46), *daily* finding in it some fresh supply for their conscience, and some new joy to their hearts.   Hence, lastly, the joy it would be to really spiritually-minded partakers of the Lord's Supper, if, ere they left the meeting and the table, the moment had come for the Lord's descending into the air, and shouting to us to meet Him at the everlasting and for ever relished marriage supper of the Lamb!   Thus linked together are the feast below and the feast above, as were the foot and the top of Jacob's ladder of old. As Paul says, when writing against all shallowness, all levity, and all self-pleasing of saints at the Lord's Supper: " For *as often* as ye eat this bread, and drink this cup, ye do show the Lord's death *till He come.*"

Blessed be God for the many assemblies of His children that in our time do each week celebrate redeeming love at the Lord's Supper. May HE give all of us grace that it may always be to our souls a " Supper " indeed, and a feast of fat things!

The Bread and the Cup.

THOSE children of God who take the Lord's Supper each "first day of the week" (Acts xx. 7), especially need to understand and keep in mind its solemnity and its responsibility. Greater frequency of partaking begets the danger of doing so too much as a habit, and therefore lightly. Indeed, there is a close connection between growth in grace, on the part of any assembly of saints, and the spirit and mode in which from week to week they partake of the Lord's Supper. Paul felt this, and connected the sad state of the saints at Corinth, with their ill ways in showing forth "the Lord's death till He come" (1 Cor. xi. 17); and in our time also a low spiritual state in an assembly will lead to its being content that "ministry of the Word" (often irrelevant, and therefore unprofitable) should delay the actual Supper to the last, instead of its being the foremost thing, and that for which the assembly met. The Lord's Supper, when scripturally kept, is so simple an action, and so brief, that it can easily be pushed aside into a mere corner of the time of meeting; but great spiritual loss is thus incurred. The very ease and brevity of taking it seated, as we rightly do, should awaken in us deep concern not to take it lightly. The Psalmist used his harp with "a solemn sound" (margin, a meditation; see Psalm xcii. 3); and surely we should with the same care partake of the emblems of Calvary's redeeming love. During their captive days in Babylon, godly Israelites refused to use their harps, or to sing Jehovah's songs, for they would not be forgetful of Jerusalem's sorrows (see Psalm cxxxvii.); and surely it were still worse in us to use the loaf and cup of the Lord's Supper, simply as an outward act, and without any leisurely or careful remembrance of Jesus' dying love!

The same may be said of the brief, yet most solemn, act of believers' baptism; but whether it is baptism, or the Lord's Supper, let each observance of either, be with ever-increasing understanding of its deep significance, and submission of soul to its Divinely-appointed authority.

In the case of the Lord's Supper, haste and lightness in partaking would be checked if the fuller and more exact teachings it conveys were sometimes dwelt on. We are by the loaf reminded: First, of our common *debt* to Him Who died for us; and secondly, of our *union* now with each other as those whom He has redeemed at such cost. The breaking of the loaf affectingly shows us how we all had part in causing Him to be "broken" for us at the cross; and the unity of the loaf reminds us that we, as partakers, are thenceforth more than ever to regard ourselves as made *one* in Him, both with each other, and also with ALL fellow-saints.

To this, we may now add a few words on the significance of the cup. Too often, perhaps, no special distinctness of meaning is seen in it, and it is regarded as conveying only the same instruction as the bread. In this, indeed, they are alike : they both set forth the same ever-precious death of our Lord. But they set it forth in different ways, and with a difference of blessing to us resulting therefrom. In one, we see the vast *number* of our *sins*, in the other the *depth* of our *sinfulness ;* and in both we learn that He gave Himself for us.

God's Word teaches us that every sinful act— whether of thought, word, or deed—of all the lives of all the Shepherd's flock, was duly laid upon the Shepherd (see Leviticus xvi. 21 ; Psalm xl. 12 ; Isaiah liii. 6, margin ; Galatians i. 4 ; Hebrews ix. 28 ; 1 Peter ii. 24, iii. 18; &c.). All these passages teach us that the full and complete *number* of our wanderings and iniquities was " made to meet " on Him ; and assembled saints express their belief of this as they break the bread, and every fragment of the loaf which they all unite to break, reminds all how truly the Lord Jesus died for each single sin that the memory and conscience of each partaker recalls to remembrance, as well as for the vastly greater number that we neither remember nor know ; for " who can understand his errors?"

Such is the deeply-affecting meaning of the *bread ;* but the *cup* has a deeper meaning still.

God's Word also teaches us that Jesus our Lord not only never sinned or transgressed, either in act, or word, or thought, but also that He had not sin *existing* in Him. He "*knew* no sin." The fountain of nature, with all its springs, which in us is essentially sinful, was in Him absolutely and Divinely pure. He was "Immanuel . . . God with us." Yet was our sinfulness reckoned to Him as if it had been His. God "made Him to be SIN for us, Who knew no sin; that we might be made the righteousness of God in Him" (2 Cor. v. 21). Also, in Romans viii. 3, 4, "God sending His own Son in the likeness of sinful flesh, and *for sin*, condemned *sin in the flesh:* that the righteousness of the law might be fulfilled in us." Again, the same chapter which says (Isaiah liii. 6), "Jehovah made the *iniquities* of us all *to meet* on Him," also says (*v.* 10), "When thou shalt make *His soul* an offering for SIN, He shall see His seed."

These passages give us a further and still deeper view of the depths of Christ's death. Inasmuch as the evil tree, that produces all the bad branches and evil fruit of man's sinful life, must needs be worse even than its products, so must it have been a deeper woe to Christ's sinless soul to be made SIN for us, even than to have our countless iniquities all numbered to Him.

As one has said, "The sufferings of His soul were the soul of His sufferings;" and it is this pouring out of "His soul" unto death that we set forth as we solemnly fill the cup at the Lord's Supper and drink it.

The previous use of the "bread" does in this way prepare us for the still more affecting use of the "wine." As we drink it, we confess that we did as truly need that our Lord should die for our sin, as for our every sinful *act*. We need to find sufficiency in His death for our foul nature, as truly as we do for the "trespasses and sins" in which we were dead; for what we WERE, as well as for what we had *done;* and this, God Himself wrought for us at Calvary, and Christ accomplished it there.

Hence our double feast of joy, and our two-fold rest in Him. We look over each fresh portion of life's journey trod, and know that its wandering steps were all borne by Him. We look within, and whilst judging ourselves with increasing self-abasement, we still know that none of the unfathomable evil of our evil hearts is kept in God's account against us, for Jesus died also for that.

Israel in the wilderness had a double supply of their need from the God that loved them. They had the manna, and also the water from the Rock, and Christ's death was typified in both those things. The minute manna, "small as the hoar frost," spread itself on the ground around their tents, the same ground on which their erring feet daily trod. But the water from the rock, springing forth at the stroke of God's rod, "gave them drink

as out of the great depths" (Psalm lxxviii. 15)—
depths too deep for eye to search, still more for
foot to tread; and Paul says, "that Rock was
Christ."

Moreover, at the Lord's Supper we " show the
Lord's death *till He come;*" and this two-fold
character of our blessing which we set forth by the
loaf and the cup, will be accomplished in all its
fulness when at His coming we sit with Him at
His table in His kingdom. For as we then shall
never, never sin or go astray again, in either deed,
or word, or thought, so also shall we then be conformed to Him *inwardly*, as well as outwardly. Sin
will then have ceased to exist in us. In that
respect, as well as in every other, " we shall be
like Him; for we shall see Him as He is."

> " To look *within* and see *no stain*,
>   Abroad no curse to trace ,
> To shed no tears, to feel no pain,
>   And see Thee face to face :
>
> " For this we're pressing onward still,
>   And in this hope would be
> More subject to the Father's will,
>   E'en now much more like Thee."

In Revelation iv., the living creatures who in
chapter v. sing of being redeemed to God by the
blood of the Lamb, are said to be " full of eyes
within," as well as " before and behind." Oh, the
love and grace of our God, which has made us His
sons and heirs, in fellowship with His Son Jesus
Christ our Lord, and will perfect us as such ! Even
so. Amen.

"Once" and "For Ever."

OUR God unites together the brief almighty *moments* in which He accomplishes His works, with the *eternal ages* in which they endure, and are both His joy and His praise. Time and eternity are His in this, as in all other ways, and as God's sons and heirs, we also can say—

> " Time and eternity are ours—
> The world, and life, and death;
> The heaven of heavens, the throne of God,
> And depths of hell beneath."

" Once " and " for ever " are expressions to remind us of two Divine realities.

" Once " points to that which is definite and precise—a thing of a day, it may be, or an hour, or a moment. It also points in Scripture to a thing finished, and needing neither addition nor repetition.

Such, for instance, was this creation. A six days' succession of almighty words spoke it into being—each utterance complete in itself, and the creation-work it effected standing in all its solidity all the " for ever " of its Divine Creator's pleasure. " He spake, and it was done; He commanded, and t stood fast " (Psalm xxxiii. 9).

Such, again, was the mighty truth that "the Word became flesh" (R.V.) His conception by the blessed virgin, through the Holy Ghost, was *one* marvellous act; but, "Immanuel," "the Man Christ Jesus," remains the Man of God's right hand—"the last Adam" "for ever"—blessed be God!

Such, too, was His glorious redemption work in death. How emphatically does the apostle, both in Romans and Hebrews, speak of that work as being only "once!" "In that He died, He died unto sin *once*." "Christ was *once* offered to bear the sins of many;" and He "entered in *once* into the holy place." How precious to our hearts and consciences is that word "*once!*" How completely it throws all the guilt and condemnation of believers in Jesus behind their backs, as they journey on to God and heaven, even as God sees it not against us before His face above! And this "once" finished work stands "*for ever*," *i.e.*, not only lastingly, as contrasted with Old Testament annual offerings; not only for our life-time, each of us, as believers; not only for all the Church's sojourn here below; but in the fullest sense of "for ever," when all the redeemed are "with the Lord;" for the Lamb "once" slain, will, by His ever-present wounds, be our title to be "for ever" with Him, and "for ever" like Him.

But "once" and "for ever" has its dark side as well as its bright one. The doom yet to be pronounced on the Christ-rejecter, will be "once" uttered; but, alas! it will stand "for ever!" "Depart, ye cursed," will need no addition nor any repetition, for the "great gulf" betwixt the rebellious and the obedient will remain "*fixed*" "for ever!" To quote Hebrews again: "It is appointed to men *once* to die; but after this the judgment," *i.e.*, the eternal judgment. Well may we say to the unsaved:—

> "Cursed by the Law, and bruised by the Fall,
> Christ hath redeemed us *once for all.*
>   'Once for all,' O sinner, believe it;
>   'Once for all,' O brother, receive it."

One more instance remains of "once" and "for ever." It is the "promise" made to us as God's sons and heirs of a "new earth and new heavens." The very setting up of Christ's great white throne will as truly banish from before it, as in a moment, this sin-stained, six days' work of creation, as all His people's sins were blotted out by the blood of His cross. But on that very throne He also says, "Behold, I make *all things* new." And His handiwork then made, stands "for ever."

Oh, may the joy of the word "once," and the strength of the word "for ever," be richly with us all our journey!

"From henceforth and for Ever."

PSALMS CXV 18; CXXI 8; CXXV. 2, CXXXI. 3.

IF "once" and "for ever" are Divine words, which, when linked together in our souls, carry much precious meaning, the kindred expression, "*From henceforth and for ever*," has also its own special instruction for us. "Once" and "for ever" tell us of the *perfection* of God's work, whatever it may be, and of how it *endures*. But "henceforth and for ever" points to the *freshness of soul* with which God's child regards these works and ways of his God, and of the joys which they increasingly inspire. God and His Word, and Christ, and all God's new creation "once" finished, eternally abide for the *eye of faith;* and *within us* the blessed Spirit unweariedly witnesses to and with our spirits. As when "God was in Christ reconciling the world unto Himself," nothing could hinder until "It is finished," was the Surety's mighty cry; so neither can the confidence of soul, which the Holy Ghost begets, ever *die* within us.

> "The flame Thy love hath kindled,
> *Shall never be put out;*
> The Spirit keeps it burning,
> Though dimmed by sin and doubt."

Faith, and hope, and love, are those living graces

that abide, more or less, in *all* believers, under all circumstances and for all time, aye, and for eternity (see 1 Corinthians xiii. 13); like the "living water," which, as a well of water, or rather, a fountain, *springs up* in the believer into everlasting life.

The Psalmist's repeated word "from henceforth" just expresses this. It matters not what may be the time or the circumstances in which it is uttered. "Henceforth" is a perpetual "NOW;" and the believer's *now* is always a confiding and triumphant one. Every such *now* becomes to him the birth-time and the starting-point for new and abiding acquaintance with God, and for fresh and enduring trust in Him and praise to Him.

Nay, more; the darker and more painful the surroundings, the more food does faith find for then and there trusting in God. The "henceforth" of submission, and of faith in God, is like the "bow in the cloud in the day of rain;" it never shines brighter, nor are its varied hues ever more distinct, than when the cloud on which they are seen is the darkest, provided only that at the same time the sun's face is shining, and the rain from heaven is falling. God's Word contains many instances of this—of faith's thriving, when mere nature would faint and die. Thus, at Ziklag, in a very dark and humbling hour, David encouraged himself in Jehovah, his God (1 Samuel xxx.); and Jonah, soon after his disobedience, could bid the mariners throw him into the sea.

So also the triumphant "henceforth and for ever" of the Psalmist, is found only in Psalms of Israel's later days, and amidst their darker surroundings. In Psalm cxv. 18, it shines out in contrast with idols that cannot deliver. Psalms cxxi., cxxv., and cxxxi., are part of the fifteen "Songs of degrees," or "of the *goings up*" from the captivity, when the feebleness, the conflicts, and the sorrows of the godly remnant were great, as we see in Ezra, Nehemiah, Haggai, and Zechariah. Yet it is in these Psalms that "henceforth and for ever" rings out, by a faith in God that overcomes the world, and that makes even the feeblest saints "more than conquerors."

"To Him be glory both NOW and for ever" (2 Peter iii. 18), and "To the only wise God our Saviour, be glory and majesty, dominion and power, both NOW and for ever" (Jude 25), are similar utterances of present triumph of soul in New Testament pages, and both stand linked with the darkest hours of waiting saints.

May grace be given us to raise "the conqueror's song" here below, always and everywhere, and in all things, even as we shall most surely ere long raise it for ever before the throne of God and of the Lamb.

"From Everlasting to Everlasting."

TIME is ours, among other things, to quicken our steps for Christ, by the lesson of its flight; and *eternity is ours* to enrich our worship even here, as it will also be our home ere long with God and the Lamb.

"From everlasting to everlasting," is an expression to show us this. In each of the four places in which we find it, it occurs in the worship of the saints: all four are in the Psalms.

It is just one of those glorious Old Testament utterances which anticipate more definite New Testament doctrine. "Grace given us in Christ Jesus," says the apostle Paul, "*before the world began*" (2 Timothy i. 9). "The God of all grace," says the apostle Peter, "who hath called us *unto His eternal glory* by Christ Jesus" (1 Peter v. 10).

Here we are plainly taught that we were loved in the eternity *past*, and that the eternity *to come* of life and glory is, by redemption, ours. Made to know this even *now*, what wonder is it that we utter our joy and praise in the above Old Testament blessed expression?

But each of the four times it occurs, it stands in a different connection.

Take, first, Psalm ciii. 15-17—

" As for man, his days are as grass :
As a flower of the field, so he flourisheth.
For the wind passeth over it, and it is gone ;
And the place thereof shall know it no more.
But the mercy of Jehovah is from *everlasting to everlasting*
Upon them that fear Him."

What joy to David to contrast this *" everlasting "* mercy with his own and others' brevity of life here ! And what joy and triumph to us to do the same !

Observe, it is " the *mercy* of Jehovah " that thus stretches from eternity to eternity. And the saved sinner, who is the subject of that mercy, knows this *now*, and worships even *now*, with at least somewhat of that wondering, boundless reverence and delight with which he will soon worship before the Throne. *Then* nothing will hinder our viewing the eternity of that mercy and love, whether in the past or the future, for the living creatures are "full of eyes *before* and *behind*," as well as " full of eyes *within* " (Rev. iv. 6); and the boundless past and future of God's love to us will be as much our study as will the thrice-holy purity of HIM before Whose Throne we shall then be standing. But Psalm. ciii. gives us the utterance of this *now* by faith.

Take, next, Psalm xc. 1, 2—

" Lord, Thou hast been our dwelling-place in all generations ;
Before the mountains were brought forth,
Or ever Thou hadst formed the earth and the world,
Even from *everlasting to everlasting*, Thou art God."

Here the believer's soul worships the *power* of our God, as in Psalm ciii. it did His *mercy ;* and the one is as eternal as the other. There it was

F

Jehovah's everlasting mercy in contrast with David's experience of the brevity of the present life of even a child of God; here Moses is considering "all the *generations*" of the godly, and how they have, at God's bidding, returned again to dust (see ver. 3, and Gen. iii. 19); but he gladly remembers that God was by faith their "dwelling-place," and that they must, *therefore*, all rise again with joy; "for He is the God of the *living*, not the God of the dead," and "all LIVE unto Him" (compare Mark xii. 26, 27).

The thousand after thousand of years, in which they lie still unraised, cannot overthrow or weaken this belief, since the GOD on Whom it is built is "*from everlasting to everlasting;*" and we, like Moses, have learned that "a thousand years in His sight" are but what "yesterday" is when it is past, or "a watch in the night;" and, therefore, we do not count the Lord "slack concerning His promise" (see 2 Peter iii. 9), though He keep His saints thousands of years in the grave waiting for their promised resurrection.

Sadducees deny the resurrection, and scoff at it; but our "hope maketh not ashamed," both because of God's *everlasting* love now shed abroad in our hearts by the Holy Ghost, and because the waiting-time of "the dead in Christ," though it has been now some six thousand years—dating from Abel onward—is so brief in the sight of HIM Who is our "dwelling-place;" for "from everlasting to everlasting Thou art GOD!"

We get the same blessed expression in Psalm
xli. 13—

" Blessed be the Lord God of Israel,
From everlasting, and to everlasting. Amen, and Amen."

Thus closes the trust and triumph of what some
have called " The sick man's Psalm." The subject
of this Psalm is bodily sickness. Verse 3 of it, has
been again and again a comfort to sick ones on
their beds; and especially when, like David in
this Psalm, they had enemies near, rather than
sympathising friends—a form of trial bitter indeed!
Job knew it; and still more did our grief-worn
blessed Lord and Master, Who quoted verse 9 as
His own (see John xiii. 18). But, both in Him
and in His people, faith triumphs when " heart
and flesh are failing," and not only rejoices at its
happy prospect (see verse 12), but begins even *now*
a worship, and a praise, which draw their fulness
from eternity itself, and says : " Blessed be the
Lord God of Israel, *from everlasting, and to everlasting.* Amen, and Amen." And, blessed be God,
it is thus in many a sick saint now !

One place of its occurrence remains (Psalm cvi.
47, 48)—

" Save us, O Lord our God,
And gather us from among the heathen,
To give thanks unto Thy holy name,
And to triumph in Thy praise.
" Blessed be the Lord God of Israel,
From everlasting to everlasting :
And let all the people say, Amen.
Praise ye the Lord."

Here, it is the same burst of praise from the whole

assembly of God's released captives, as it was from the sick saint's individual chamber ; and the measure in which they have proved His goodness, only makes them still more cry, " Gather us from among the nations," that we may " triumph in Thy praise ; " for many remain still ungathered, and the theme of their worship reaches beyond all bounds of time, and stretches from eternity to eternity. " Man is of few days," it is true, " and full of trouble," and God's dear children are no exception to this rule ; but whether it be David in Psalms ciii. and xli., or Moses in Psalm xc., or the re-gathered exiles of Psalm cvi. ; all generations of saints, and still more we of these " last days," can, and do, "*joy in God,* through our Lord Jesus Christ, by Whom we have *now* received the reconciliation."

> " On earth the song begins,
>   In heaven more sweet and loud :
>   To Him Who cleansed our sins
>   In His atoning blood ;
>   To Him we sing in joyful strain,
>   Be honour, power, and praise.   Amen."

"Them That Fear Him."

SAINTS have had before them often the blessed *fulness* of Psalm ciii., as shown by the frequency in it of the word "ALL" (*vv.* 1, 2, 3, 6, 19, 21, 22); but in studying this precious Psalm, notice should also be taken of the threefold recurrence of the words, "them that fear Him." The one utterance fits well to the other. For if the frequency of the word "ALL" shows the *fulness* of blessing dwelt on and aimed at in the Psalm, the expression "them that fear Him" reminds us that no fulness of blessing from God can be effectual, either *for* us or *in* us, except as by His grace we are amongst "them that fear Him." The heavens may be "black with clouds," and there may be "a great rain" from "the God of ALL grace," but of what avail is it to the soil beneath unless the clods of the ground have been broken and opened to let it in? In Hebrews vi. 7, the apostle says that only such earth as "*drinketh in* the rain that cometh oft upon it," really "receives blessing from God;" and thus he distinguishes between God's own children and mere professors. Surely this element in

us of godly, filial fear, is God's own way of causing
our souls to drink in the rain of His grace and His
blessing.   Hence it is that so much is said of "the
fear of the Lord" in both Old Testament and New.

Like every other Divine grace, it is found in
God's children in different degrees, even as it was
found in our blessed Lord Himself in Divine fulness
and without measure (see Isaiah xi. ; and Hebrews
v. 7).   Psalm cxxx. 4, reminds us that this filial fear
of the Lord originates in us from the knowledge of
His grace and love towards us.   It springs out of
our having redemption in Christ, "even the forgiveness of sins according to the riches of His
grace."   How naturally, and how fitly, therefore,
does the apostle say to believing "servants" in
Ephesians vi. 5, "Servants, be obedient to them that
are your masters according to the flesh, *with* FEAR
and trembling, in singleness of your heart, *as unto
Christ.*"   Such a state of mind, Godward, is lacking
in the daily life of too many children of God, and we
need the exhortation of Psalm xxxiv. : " O *fear* the
Lord, ye His saints " (*v.* 9), and also instruction,
according to verse 11 : " I will *teach* you the fear of
the Lord."

But the believer must pursue for himself the whole
blessed subject of " the fear of the Lord " as found
in the entire Word of God.   Let us now turn to the
three occurrences of it in Psalm ciii.   Each time it
stands in a different connection.

In verses 10, 11, it stands linked with the abundance of God's *mercy* towards us respecting our *sins* and *iniquities*. And as to these, the Psalmist says, "As the heaven is high above the earth, so great is His mercy toward *them that fear Him.*" This was the fountain-head and beginning of our acquaintance with God, viz., the "abundant mercy," as Peter calls it, by which we were "begotten again" when first we believed. And on that happy day, we first took our place amongst "them that fear Him." And this way and means of knowing His fear remains with us all our days; for to the last it is true, by His same "abundant mercy," that as we confess our sins, " HE is faithful and just to forgive us our sins, and to cleanse us from all unrighteousness."

But in verses 13, 14, compassion for our *weakness* and remembrance of the feebleness of our *bodily frame* is the subject; and here also the Psalmist says, " Like as a father pitieth His children, so Jehovah pitieth *them that fear Him :* for He knoweth our frame ; He remembereth that we are dust." It is this mindfulness of our infirmity, as well as provision for our sins, that especially shows the perfection of God's love to us as His children. It is like the minuteness with which our Lord took care there should be *"much grass"* in the place in which He bade the multitude sit down, that He might feed them. Or it reminds us of our great High Priest being from actual personal experience touched with the feeling of our infirmity, as well as

able to show Himself and His wounds in heaven
on behalf of our *sins*. These evidences of a
thoughtful and absolutely *perfect* love, first beget,
and next deepen in us, that loving and filial *fear*
of Him, of which the Psalmist speaks. And this
child-like fear of the Lord commends us but the
more to His regard and His affection each day and
hour He finds it in us.

Our God on His part says, " The Lord taketh
pleasure in them that fear Him, in those that hope
in His mercy " (Ps. cxlvii. 11), and *we* say to Him :

> " Oh, let Thy fear within me dwell,
>   Thy love my footsteps guide;
> That fear shall all vain fears expel,
>   That love all loves beside."

The third and last place is verses 15-17 : " As for
man, his days are as grass: as a flower of the field,
so he flourisheth. For the wind passeth over it,
and it is gone ; and the place thereof shall know it
no more. But the mercy of the Lord is from everlasting to everlasting upon *them that fear Him*."
Here we see the fear of the Lord pointing us on to
resurrection. Not sins and iniquities form the
subject here, nor even our living infirmities only;
but death itself is in view. The place that has
known us is seen as knowing us *no more ;* but the
" mercy of our Lord Jesus Christ unto eternal life,"
as Jude expresses it, is the portion of " them that
fear Him."

Thus did Old Testament saints, in their early
day, look away from time and sense into eternal

realities, even before Christ's death and resurrection, and before the Holy Ghost had come down to fashion God's children into one body and one building. For they were amongst "them that fear Him," and this blessed grace granted to them enabled them to see our God as One forgiving all their iniquities, and feeling for their infirmities; and also as One Whose mercy, being "from everlasting to everlasting," must also raise them from the dead, and give them glory. Thus Abraham "looked for a city . . . whose Maker and Builder is God." Thus Moses "had respect unto the recompense of the [heavenly] reward." Thus David testified of a risen One Who should "no more return to corruption" (Psalm xvi. 10.) Thus, too, Job spoke of a kinsman Redeemer who should "stand at the latter day over his dust" (see Hebrew), and by Whose resurrection power he should in his flesh "see God;" and his reins within him were consumed with longing for that day. All these were amongst "them that fear Him," and were such as kept His covenant, and remembered His "commandments to do them;" for "the fear of the Lord is *clean*," as well as "enduring for ever" (see Psalm xix. 9). Such were all Old Testament saints, in some measure, and according to the light then vouchsafed; and such, too, by His grace to us, are we all of this more favoured dispensation. But oh! to have this humble, happy, and filial fear of the Lord increase in us!

"Visit" and "Visitation."

"This I say, brethren, the time is short."
(1 CORINTHIANS vii. 29.)

L ET us look at the words "visit" and "visitation" in some of the places in which they
occur in the New Testament,* and the
Holy Ghost's use of them will be found to
teach the same lesson of the *brevity* of the Church's
sojourn here below, and, as a consequence, the
diligent and heavenly mind she ought to show.

First, our blessed Lord's birth amongst us, and
all His life and work, are spoken of as but a
visiting of mankind, not a dwelling among them.
Inspired Zacharias said, when his son, John the
Baptist, was born as Christ's forerunner, "Blessed
be the Lord God of Israel; for He hath *visited* and
redeemed His people" (Luke i. 68); and when his
newly-loosened and enraptured tongue went on to
tell of the Christ Himself, he spoke of "the tender
mercy of our God, whereby the Dayspring from on
high hath *visited* us" (*v.* 78). Compare also
John i. 14: "The Word was made flesh, and

---

* In the Old Testament the words "visit" and "visitation" are
solemnly used of the judgment and wrath of God, as they are of His
mercy in the New. See especially Jeremiah vi. 15; viii. 12; ix. 25
(margin); x. 15; xi. 23; xxiii. 12, &c.

tabernacled among us" (see Greek). And surely
a visiting of men is the very expression suitable;
for two things are implied in a *visit*—one, that it is
the arrival to you of one from another place; and
the other, that it is only for a little while, and not
for a life-long stay. And how true were both
these things of the " sunrising" that shone from
the Bethlehem manger on both Judæan and
Galilean darkness !

Nor was this expression used only by the tongue
of prophecy at His birth; but when He came forth
anointed by the Spirit for public ministry, and
Isaiah's words were fulfilled—" The people that
sat in darkness saw great light" (Isaiah ix. 2)—
our blessed Master so hasted on from town to
town, and village to village, like the sun in its
daily course, that the very people themselves used
concerning Him the same expression, after He
had raised to life the widow of Nain's son: " A
fear came on all: and they glorified God, saying,
. . . God hath *visited* His people" (Luke vii. 16).

Yes; the light from on high shone at Nain, and
sent its life-beams into the eyeballs of the dead,
and into the sorrow-darkened heart of the widowed
mother; but as, like the sun in the heavens, " He
could not be hid" (Mark vii. 24), so also, like the
sun, He could not be, and would not be, held back
in His course, nor even delayed. Death, with its
arrows, its scythe, and its unsparing foot, was
moment by moment advancing and at work; and

HE, "the Light of Life," must not be idle. All is movement in the scene at Nain. Death had been busy—had before made the mother a widow, and had now carried off her son, and he was being borne to the grave. But Jesus was on *His* way. He had just left Capernaum, and as the One " Who *went about* doing good" (see Acts x. 38), He left at Nain this footprint of power and blessing as He passed on.

Once more in Luke's Gospel this kind of word occurs : " Thou (O Jerusalem) knewest not the time of thy *visitation*" (see Luke xix. 44)—a most affecting passage ! The light that had shone out from Jesus " in the days of His flesh "—" the Day-spring from on high " which dawned at Bethlehem, and had shone over Galilee and Samaria and Judæa—was now sinking to its west ; the brief day of their Messiah in their midst was about to close, and it was shadowed already by the dark inter-cepting cloud of their murderous hate. Calmly and sorrowfully does He tell them they had not known " the time of their *visitation*."

God's "righteous Servant" had ever had a " single eye," and His body had always been " full of light " (Luke xi. 34, 36), and this light had shone out. Jesus had Himself said of His own steps below, " Are there not twelve hours in the day ?" (John xi. 9) and not an hour nor moment of His appointed course had He ceased both to move and to shine. " Yet a little while is the Light among

you," had been His cry; " walk while ye have the
Light, lest darkness come upon you " (John xii.
35); but all had been in vain as regards Jerusalem
and the nation as a whole, and Christ's affecting
lament over them points to what the *onward*
character of His ministry amongst them had been.
It was, says He, "the time of thy *visitation.*"
Their scribes had said, " Elias must first come "
(see Matthew xvii. 10); and, like " children sitting
in the market-place "—mere idlers—they had
willingly listened to the dreams of these false
dreamers, and had taken no warning from the diligent haste of the Son of God in their midst. In
vain had Zacharias prophesied that "the Day-
spring from on high " would, like the sun, make
but a *visit*—in vain had the admiring crowd themselves once said, " God hath *visited* His people "—
Israel had taken no warning, and the shades of
evening were on them, and they were indeed without excuse; for HE who had untiringly journeyed
and wrought and preached amongst them, now
wept over the city as He beheld it, saying, " If
thou hadst known, even thou, at least in this *thy
day*, the things which belong unto thy peace! but
now they are hid from thine eyes."

But these same two words, " visit " and " visitation," are used by the Holy Ghost of the CHURCH's
life here below, and of *her* ministry, as we have
seen they are of our Lord's. It was when the
Church was assembled at Jerusalem to take

counsel as to her work in the earth for God and
for Christ (see Acts xv.), that Peter told of the
blessing of Cornelius's house by his means, and
James added: " Simeon hath declared how God at
the first did VISIT the Gentiles, to take out of
them a people for His name." This one expression marks out the Church's present work
among men.   It is not to set up anything national,
nor even to tarry, or to loiter amongst men at all ;
but to accomplish the *" visit"* on which she is sent
to the nations, somewhat as our Master accomplished His to Israel as His own people.   " He
came unto His own [things], and His own
[people] received Him not." We are sent by
God on but a *visit* to the nations of the earth, for
His glory, and to gather a people out of them.
Did we but more remember this, as evangelists,
how separate it would keep us from the world in
which we are labouring ! and also, how it would
even more hasten us than the flight of time does, to
do diligently our heavenly business of proclaiming
to men the blessed Gospel this *"little while"* we
have for it !

The pastor's and teacher's work is to have this
same thought of brevity and heavenly haste in it
as the evangelist's ; for Paul said to Barnabas in
the same chapter, " Let us go again and *visit* our
brethren in every city where we have preached
the word of our Lord, and see how they do "
(Acts xv. 36).   We know in their *visits* of business,

or of friendship, or of sightseeing, how much men exert themselves and do, warned by the shortness of their opportunity. If we more saw that "NOW is the accepted time; NOW is the day of salvation," how like them we should be in this respect!

But the word "visitation" also is used to show the brevity of our time on earth as saints and witnesses for Christ. The very Peter who spoke in Acts xv., says in his first Epistle (ii. 11, 12): "Dearly beloved, I beseech you as strangers and pilgrims, abstain from fleshly lusts, which war against the soul; having your conversation honest" (*i.e.*, conduct befitting) "among the Gentiles: that . . . they may by your good works, which they shall behold, glorify God in the day of *visitation*." Peter, as a Jew, was once looking for an earthly kingdom with Christ, and for things established here, and made permanent; but he now sees himself and his fellow-saints as "begotten again unto a living hope," and both houseless and nationless on earth ("strangers and pilgrims"), whose business is to give such a testimony "amongst the Gentiles" as that, in this brief "day of visitation," they may be led to "glorify God;" and to this end, says the apostle, "I beseech you, abstain from fleshly lusts"—first, because they war against your own souls; and second, that your good works and pilgrim ways may be manifest, and show men the brevity of their present day of Gospel grace, and thus win them for Christ.

Such testimony is the most powerful of any.
Bunyan says that the *passing on* of Christian and
Faithful through Vanity Fair, as those who could
not be detained in it, together with their unworldly
gear and ways, set all the fair in a hubbub. Oh
for a like testimony in us as God's Church and
God's saints, in this world and in these days!
God Himself is not ashamed to be called the God
of such; for they declare plainly that they seek a
country (a fatherland; see Greek); and the country
they desire is a heavenly one, and to it they are
hastening. The haste of the waiting saints to
fulfil their mission, and to reach their home, and to
reign with Christ, should be such as to warn men
of the brevity of their Gospel season, even more
loudly than does the flight of time.

True, ours is but a borrowed light; it is not like
Immanuel's, a "sunrising" (see Luke i. 78,
margin). But in His absence, we should, like the
moon, draw our light from Him, and should shine
it on men's darkness "till He come." The moon,
as Job expresses it, "walking in brightness" (Job
xxxi. 26), gives "light upon the earth;" and
though the "lesser light," it nevertheless "rules
the night" (see Genesis i. 16); and such should
the Church of God be among men. But in order
to give her light to all, the moon no more loiters
than does the sun. Course after course she keeps,
her movement as punctual as his, though not as
swift. Oh that it had been thus with past suc-

cessive generations of God's waiting saints! Oh
that it might yet be thus with us who are alive and
remain!

Moses, ere he departed, pronounced on the
Joseph tribe the blessing not only of " the precious
fruits brought forth by the *sun*," but also of "the
precious things put forth by the *moons*" (see
Hebrew); as if he would say, In Joseph's tents let
there be no moon that does not " walk in brightness," and "rule the night" by "giving its light
upon the earth." And though the loving elo-
quence of Moses failed to preserve Israel as a light
for God, because she forgot her Naziariteship, and
defiled it, let us be waked up as "the Israel of
God" (Galatians vi. 16) of this present time; for
" moons " won't wait for the sleepers, nor yet for
the drunkards, of the night. We must as much
use them while we have them as our blessed
Master did the "twelve hours" of the day given
Him by His Father and our Father, and His God
and our God.

G

"The Coming One."

IN both Old and New Testaments, "the Coming One" stands out as one of the many blessed titles of our Lord; and in this world of sin and sorrow it is

> "A name He bears,
> And a form of love He wears,"

most joyful to Himself, and most comforting to His people who are here below waiting for Him. It was so to Old Testament saints in the character of the coming in which they were waiting for Him, and verily it is so to us. Our "heavenly calling," with its brighter hope, and the deeper troubles and darker guilt of the present age, unite to make the very name, "the Coming One," dear to us. In the original Hebrew and Greek it reads more plainly as a *title* of our Lord than it does in our English translation.

The much-loved verse, Hebrews x. 37, "For yet a little while, and *He that shall come* will come, and will not tarry," should rather be, "and *The Coming One* (ὁ ἐρχομενος) will come." "The Coming One," He was in the thoughts and hearts of all those who, Anna-like, of old looked for the redemption of Jerusalem; and "the Coming One"

He still is to *our* thoughts and hearts, though in such a different way and for such a different work. Not again, as then, "to put away sin by the sacrifice of Himself," but "unto them that look for Him shall He appear the second time without sin" (*i.e.*, without sin-offering) "unto salvation." But in either case the title of "the Coming One" suits Him.

And as the Spirit in the saints uses it here below, it is but the response to *His own utterance* above. "Sacrifice and offering Thou wouldest not, but a body hast Thou prepared me. . . . Then said I, Lo, I come to do Thy will, O God." This was His language before He came to suffer and die; and in our New Testament time He still says, "I will come again, and receive you unto Myself." Surely the Spirit and the Bride's crying "Come," is but the worthy and the suited worship of Him whose very title is "the Coming One."

Some passages in which this title may be fairly said to occur, may now be pointed out; and first in the Old Testament. "Blessed be He that cometh" (or "the Coming One," see Hebrew), "in the Name of the Lord" (Psalm cxviii. 26). This verse may be taken as expressing the hope of the godly in the Israel nation. They looked for "the Coming One" as a matter of deliverance, and of joy and blessing. The darker their troubles were —whether national or individual, or in family life —the more they *leaned hard* upon the expectation of "the Coming One." The 118th Psalm shows this. It was written at a time of some deliverance, but tells of waiting for still more; and the cry (*v.* 25), "Save now, I beseech Thee, O Jehovah," is instantly, as it were, answered to the sorrowing heart by the next words, " Blessed be the Coming One in the name of Jehovah." Thus inwoven was this title with every bright and blessed expectation that the godly ones in Israel cherished. From the moment of the promise of the woman's Seed in Eden's garden, faith and hope alike looked *onward* —Abraham, to the Lamb that God *would* provide; Moses, to the Prophet that *should arise* after him; David, to the Son Who should be *heir* of his throne for ever; the prophets, to the Suffering One Who was the subject of their own utterances; and here in Psalm cxviii. the returned remnant from the Babylon captivity still say, " Blessed be the Coming One "—till it is left to Simeon in the Temple to say at last, " Now lettest Thou Thy servant depart in peace : for mine eyes have seen Thy salvation." " The Coming One " was indeed then "what kings and prophets waited for;" and the darker grew the shades around them, the dearer did this title of their Messiah become to them.

But the Old Testament has *warning words* on the subject of "the Coming One," as well as the language of hope and joy. We find it in such Scriptures as Malachi iii. 1, 2 : " The Lord, Whom ye seek " (*i.e.*, formally and hypocritically seek),

" shall suddenly COME to His temple . . . behold, He shall COME . . . But who may abide
the day *of His coming?* and who shall stand when
He appeareth ?" We here have the *solemn* aspect
of that day of " the Coming One," as we before
had its joyous aspect. The state of the nation
required it. Their use of the 118th Psalm in the
Synagogue and Temple was always helping them to
the laxest and most carnal repetitions of, " Blessed
be the Coming One in the name of Jehovah."
Psalms cxiii.-cxviii. formed in Jewish usage " the
greater Hallel " (answering to the prayer-book of a
modern national religion), and thus it was sung at
the annual festivals, especially at the Passover and
the Feast of Tabernacles. Hence its closing words
would remain in the ear and memory of a people
who had but few copies of their Scriptures in their
own dwellings, and the most careless Israelite
would carry away the words, " Blessed be the
Coming One," and use them as a mere chorus of
the song. Thus it was that even the Samaritan
woman at the well could say, " I know that
Messias *cometh* . . . when He is *come*, He
will tell us all things "—all careless and immoral
though she was. No wonder, then, that prophets
gave warnings of that day, as godly Psalmists also
sang of it. The very title, " The Coming One,"
was the highest joy of the righteous, and the most
awful warning to formalists and hypocrites.

The same double application of this title of our

Lord is in the New Testament. There John the
Baptist is the first to use it. See Matthew iii. 11 :
" I indeed baptise you with water unto repentance :
but He that cometh after me " (or, "*the Coming
One* after me ") " is mightier than I . . . He
shall baptise you with the Holy Ghost, and with
fire . . . He will . . . gather His wheat
into the garner; but He will burn up the chaff
with unquenchable fire." Here we again have the
two opposite aspects of "the Coming One." To
the submitting and trusting sinner, "the Coming
One" brings the joy and blessing of the Holy
Ghost, and heavenly fire—a " fire " that is kindled
already in the souls of saved sinners, but will be
perfected both *in* them and *around* them when
they stand in God's own presence on the "sea of
glass *mingled with fire* . . . having the harps
of God." But John the Baptist warns the religious formalists, as Malachi did before him, that
the day of "the Coming One" could bring them
nothing but that "unquenchable fire" which would
consume them as chaff.

But this faith in "the Coming One," and testimony concerning Him, both to saint and sinner,
needs to be *sustained* in our souls, for prolonged
sufferings will severely test it. We see this in
Matthew xi. 3, the next place where the title
occurs. The same John, who had, at the outset of
his public ministry, testified so blessedly of Jesus
as "the Coming One," was now cast into prison,

and, surrounded by every discouragement, his faith wavers, and he sends two of his disciples to Jesus with the question, " Art thou He that should come " (or, " Art thou the Coming One ?"), " or do we look for another ?" Who that listened to John's words at the bank of the Jordan would ever have expected this ? Let all of us watch and pray ; for, as our Master kindly said, " The spirit is willing, but the flesh is weak." And especially do we need this watchfulness and prayer to keep alive in our hearts the hope of " The Coming One," and our steadfast testimony to Jesus our Lord in this character. But John the Baptist had brought his drooping faith and hope to the right source for help ; and perhaps no part of his Saviour's answer would more revive these graces in him than the word, " The poor have the Gospel preached unto them." And so with us. It is patient ministry to " the poor of the flock," and Gospel labour to the perishing around us, which so helps to revive in us the confident expectation of " The Coming One," and keeps it alive ; whilst he who smites his fellow-servants with hard words—whether written and printed, or only spoken—and eats and drinks with the drunken, is the one who really says in his heart, " My Lord delayeth His coming."

But John the Baptist in prison is not the only one in the New Testament who thus fainted and grew weary as to " The Coming One." Paul had to speak to the Hebrews in the same strain as Jesus did to His ill-treated forerunner. The Hebrews were no longer *building themselves up* upon their " most holy faith," as they had formerly done, and were not holding fast the profession of their hope; they were acting as if He who had promised that He would " come again " was not faithful. They began to think that confession of the Nazarene, " the carpenter's son," and going forth unto Him " outside the camp " of the national religion, was costing them too dear. They no longer " took joyfully the spoiling of their goods," for Jesus' sake, as they once did. Thus faith no longer grasped the " better and enduring substance " which they had in Jesus at God's right hand; and their hearts no longer sang,

> " The road may be rough,
> But it *cannot* be *long*."

It seemed to them both long and rough. Like John the Baptist in the prison, they were fainting under severe and lengthened trial; but Paul points to Jesus as " the Coming One," and says, " Ye have need of patience, that after ye have done the will of God, ye might receive the promise; for yet a little while, and ' THE COMING ONE ' will come, and will not tarry." Thus it is again to fainting saints that the Holy Ghost gives this precious title of our Lord. Here also, as in Matthew iii., it is accompanied with a warning word of the " perdition" of those who " draw back," and thus show they never were Christ's.

There is yet another sense of Jesus our Lord, as " The Coming One." It is found in the Book of the Revelation. (See Revelation i. 8, and iv. 8.) " I am Alpha and Omega, the beginning and the ending, saith the Lord, which is, and which was, *and which is to come* (or, " and the Coming One "), " the Almighty." And again, " Holy, holy, holy, Lord God Almighty, which was, and is, *and is to come* " (or, " and art the Coming One "). This shows us God and the Lamb as still to us " the Coming One," even in the glory. For *faith*, which rests in Him as our present portion, and *hope*, which is ever expecting future good things from Him, not yet received, are as eternally abiding as love itself is. " Now *abideth* faith, hope, love these three." (1 Corinthians xiii. 13.) It is in this sense that Jesus our Lord will *for ever* be to us the One that is " to come." There is a sense in which we shall still for ever say,

" 'Tis better on before."

More heights, and depths, and lengths, and breadths of boundless blessedness will still remain stored up for us in God, and in the Lamb! Do not the very words, " The Lamb which is in the midst of the throne shall FEED them, and shall LEAD them unto fountains of living waters," imply pastures ever new, and springs deeper than ever before tasted, with which it will be His eternal joy to acquaint His redeemed?

If so, the Scripture teaches three different

unfoldings of Jesus to the faith and hope of His people as "the Coming One"—one *in the past*, as "the Coming One" Who should one day put away sin by the sacrifice of Himself; another *now*, "the Coming One" Who shall ere long call us to Himself in the image of the heavenly; and another that lasts for ever; for when bearing His own heavenly image, we still shall joy in Him as the Lord God Almighty, Who not only was and is, but is *to come*.

Well may Solomon say, " It is the glory of God to *conceal* a thing: but the honour of kings is to search out a matter" (Proverbs xxv. 2); for it is surely true that to all eternity, there will be more blessedness *hidden* in God and the Lamb than any of us His saints will ever know; and our "honour," who are His kings and priests, will for ever be to " search " it out.

.May this be more our business even now. Amen.

"The End of all Things."

1 Peter iv. 7-11.

WE may well hail the growing nearness to us both of our Lord's return and of His millennial reign, and of that final new earth and new heavens which shall remain for ever. And equally ought we to stir each other to abound but the more in works of faith and love, and, as Peter says in the verses above quoted, to be "sober, and watch unto prayer" (see Greek).

In the course of his epistle, Peter has been glancing into the ages past. He has noted the prophets testifying beforehand "the sufferings of Christ, and the glories which should follow," and who prophesied of that very salvation which has now come to us by the Holy Ghost sent down from heaven (see 1 Peter i. 10-12); he has spoken also of the preaching of even Noah's time, and the similarity of it to God's testimony now (1 Peter iii. 19, 20); and he has declared that the continuous aim of the Gospel in every age has been that men might be righteously condemned who have rejected it, and that those who are blessed by it might live

here below, "according to God in the Spirit."
"But the end of all things," he next says, "is at
hand;" _i.e._, these fulfillings of the Old Testament
prophets by the preaching of those whom the Holy
Ghost, come down from heaven, now strengthens
to preach (compare also Romans i. 2, and xvi. 25, 26),
will not last much longer; and the solemn and
godly actings of this testimony in condemning its
rejectors, and bringing to God, and to salvation
and godliness, such as welcome it—this will not
last much longer. "The end of all things is at
hand." The past ages cannot be gone over again,
and even in this present age, which is to faith's view
the shortest of any—for it is only a time of VISITING
the Gentiles, so very short that it is spoken of as
"the _hour_ that now is" (John iv. 23, and v. 25)—
has the sands of its hour-glass nearly run out.
The Gospel rejecters—of whom he says, "What
shall the _end_ be?"—have not much longer for their
scorning; and the patient and suffering witnesses
for Christ have not much longer to wait and to
endure. Who can wonder that the aged apostle
adds, "Be ye therefore sober, and watch unto
prayer?"

Nor does he exhort to prayers only, but (_v._ 8) to
that LOVE to all saints which, like a mantle, has
sufficient width and size in it to enable you to love
them all, spite of "a multitude of sins" in them;
and (_v._ 9) that diligence too, as well as love, which
makes us watch, as Abraham did at his tent door,

just before Sodom perished, for opportunities of
showing " hospitality without grudging," hastening
to show ourselves " good stewards of the manifold
grace of God," the little while that remains,
whether it be in things of doctrine, or of this life's
goods (*vv.* 10, 11).

And all this with a view to God in all things
being " glorified through Jesus Christ, to whom be
praise and dominion for ever and ever. Amen."
Truly the Apostle's spirit flows on along with the
words of his pen, and he seems in his own soul to
reach the glorious close.

But though so near the end, there was time
enough even yet for a " fiery trial," which was to
try them (*vv.* 12-19); and so there may be time
enough now. " Ten days " was time enough to test
the Smyrna Church (see Revelation ii. 10).

But the blessed " END " before us makes us count
all the suffering, and the " grief that intervenes,"
as not worthy to be compared with that " END " of
our faith which we have already received, " even
the salvation of our souls " (1 Peter i. 9).

All truth is summed up and shines forth in Jesus
Himself; and He is our " END," as He also is our
" beginning." Thrice, He thus declares Himself in
the Book of Revelation. " I am the beginning and
the end," is His own word. In Revelation i. 8, in connection with His Churches, both as to their present
state, and their day of crowning; in Rev. xxii. 13,
in connection with that holy city, the bride, and

her fulfilment of her millennial day of reigning with Him over this earth below ; and once more, in Revelation xxi. 6, as to that perfected new creation of new heavens and new earth, when the final blessed "It is done" shall reveal Jesus as God's "END" for ever in sabbatic rest and joy, and as our "END" also of salvation and blessing fully accomplished.

Well may we both sing, and also watch and pray, as we cry to each other—" The end of all things is at hand."

Oh, that for the Bridegroom watching,
    As becomes the ransom'd Bride,
Jesus' word of patience keeping,
    We did in His love abide.

We that shall appear with Jesus,
    In His glorious beauty clad,
Fain would now be wise to please Thee,
    Wise to make our Father glad.

Thou, the living God, art resting,
    In Thy Son, the spotless Lamb ;
We with Him in song uniting,
    Magnify Thy holy name.

R. C. Chapman.

In Memoriam:

Mr. HENRY DYER.

"God took him." *November 15th, 1896.*

O RAPTUR'D worshipper!
   Our hearts would follow thee within the vail,
As wrapped in wonder, first thine eyes beheld,
Without a cloud between, thy glorious Lord!
What were thy feelings then? Say, did thy speech
(On earth so ready) find a fitting word
To make thy heart's full adoration known?
Or low in solemn silence didst thou bow—
Silence more eloquent than oral speech—
Before the LAMB once slain on Calvary?

Well we remember with what rev'rence thou
On earth didst worship at His sacred feet:
And with what mingled feelings—joy and grief—
Thy spirit contemplated Calvary's woe!
But who shall tell what that glad moment wrought
Within thy breast, when thou didst see His face,
And on thine ears Heaven's sacred *Hallel* fell?
That song had oft on earth entranced thy soul,
But with what holy rapture thou wouldst haste
To join the anthem and to swell His praise!

While in the body pent *our* spirits are,
Mem'ry will oft recall the sacred hour
When round the hallowed Table of our Lord,
In sweet communion, thou didst lead our souls
In worship low to bow before the throne.

Brother, belov'd and longed for, we shall miss
Thy saintly service in the Church below!
Vig'rous in mind, and strong in soul wast thou—
Like fiery steeds which Pharaoh's chariot drew,
So were they as compared to thy frail flesh.

Thy sacrifice of self, thy zealous love,
Endeared thee to our hearts in either sphere,
Yet not one moment would we bring thee back;
With patient expectation we would watch,
And wait the mighty Voice which soon shall call
To union everlasting with our God.

                                        M. M. D.

    Leominster.

QUIET WATERS

OF REST AND REFRESHING.

The Cross of Christ.

IT is unspeakably precious and blessed to know
that the all-important question of salvation and
peace with God is settled by simple faith in the
Lord Jesus Christ, as having been delivered up
for our offences, and raised again on account of our
justification by His blood. This effected, the next
important subject is *fellowship with God* in the
path of obedience to His word—a fellowship that
grows by increasing acquaintance with His truth.

For this growth we are as dependent on God as
for life; dependent on the teaching of the Holy
Ghost to enable us to discover not only the truths
of Scripture, but the place assigned to each, and
its relative importance to other truths, in order
that they may occupy a corresponding place in our
minds, hearts, and ways. Lacking this, our growth

B

will be distorted, and we shall neither have spiritual strength nor comeliness.

Whatever is presented to our faith in the Word of God is *essential;* for that which is not essential to salvation from hell, is essential to full obedience and communion.

There is one truth to which these remarks especially apply. It is that presented to us by the little word with which we are so familiar—"*The Cross.*"

Often is this word repeated in Scripture, because of its importance; oftener still by the lips of old and young around us, being sometimes spoken or sung without thought, without faith, and without heart—a solemn mockery to God; often, too, through grace, with deep thought, faith, and love; but even then, it is not fully understood nor properly valued. Indeed, he who understands its meaning best, and feels its value most deeply, will be the first to say, "How little I know!"

Thousands now wear a crucifix attached to their neck-ribbon or watch, made of gold, silver, steel, or bone, whose state of soul, and worldly, sinful life, proclaim their utter ignorance of that which is meant in Scripture by the word "cross;" the out-side symbol usually indicating either the absence of the reality, or the scanty and imperfect know-ledge of its worth and power.

What, then, does the Holy Ghost mean when He uses the term "The cross of Christ?"

When speaking of it in the Gospels, He refers to the material instrument of torture which Jesus carried, to which He was transfixed by the wicked hands of His enemies, and on which He died. Again, when He records the loving act of Joseph and Nicodemus in taking down His body from the cross, He means the same, but never attaches any sacred power or any virtue to the wood. He simply records the facts. But when using the term afterwards, either to show its mighty work, to present its teachings, or illustrate its practical power, He does not mean by the "cross" the instrument of death, but the depth of humiliation to which He Who hung on it descended, the nature of the death He suffered thereon, and its power with God for men. I say WITH GOD, for the Divine, Godward aspect of the cross, although not always, nor even generally, first discerned by the sinner, is the primary aspect, and man's benefit the secondary.

Shall I say that Abraham understood this when he answered Isaac's pertinent, piercing, soul-stirring question : " Where is the lamb for a burnt offering?" It might be too much to say he understood it ; but not so that the Holy Ghost, who knew it, dictated the answer, and fitted to his lips the words, " GOD will provide HIMSELF the lamb for a burnt offering." He might have said, God will provide a lamb, or provide for *us* a lamb ; but " *Elohim* will provide HIMSELF THE LAMB " was the proper answer, and therefore the answer given.

Yes, the Son of God made flesh—the Word incarnate, born to die the sacrificial, atoning death of the cross, is God's provision for the display of His own glory in the salvation of sinners.

It may be well now to examine a few Scriptures in which the cross is mentioned; and may the Holy Ghost help me to write, and also make profitable to the reader that which may be written.

First, let me call attention to some of those Scriptures in which the work of the cross or the virtues of the death of Jesus on it are presented. I observe this order because it is God's order. The Holy Ghost never presents Christ in the moral glory of His life for *imitation*, until the sinner knows the value of His death and resurrection for *salvation* and *peace;* in other words, the Spirit never presents Christ as a pattern, until He has been received by faith as a *Saviour.*

There are passages of Scripture in which the work of the *cross* and the blessed results of Christ's death are described, but the word itself does not occur in them; while there are others presenting the same truth by means of the word "cross."

Of the former are such passages as these: "Whom God hath set forth, a propitiation through faith in His *blood;*" "Who was *delivered* for our offences;" "When we were enemies we were reconciled to God by the *death* of His Son;" "He hath *made* Him to be *sin* for us, Who knew no sin;" "Who *gave Himself* for our sins;" "In Whom we have redemption through His *blood*, the forgiveness of sins." Of the latter are such as: "That He might reconcile both unto God in one body by the *cross;*" "Having made peace through the blood of His *cross;*" "Nailing it to His *cross;*" "Who for the joy that was set before Him endured the *cross.*'

In these and similar Scriptures, the Holy Ghost presents to faith the blessed work of covering of sin (atonement), reconciliation to God, the fulfilling of prophecies and of types as to the bearing away of sin, the meeting of all the claims of justice, effecting perfect, eternal deliverance from guilt and condemnation by the death of Christ, the spotless Lamb of God, on the tree. This is our *gain*, not the *material cross.*

In all this blessed work of the cross the mind of God is declared and His character revealed. Jehovah proclaimed His Name to Moses when hidden in the cleft of the rock and covered with His hand; but it was in connection with the *second* pair of tables, which were deposited in the ark and covered with the mercy-seat, on which and before which was sprinkled the blood that covered sin. There Moses learned Jehovah's Name, and saw that which might then be seen of Him and of His glory.

The cross also instructs us. It teaches those who are saved by its work. Jesus crucified proclaims the *love* of God: "Herein is love, not that we loved God, but that He loved us, and sent His Son, the propitiation for our sins."

If the act of God in giving His Son and delivering Him up to death for us teaches us His love, the sufferings of that Son, when made a curse for us, reflect equally the holiness and justice of the God of love. God is holy, and cannot behold iniquity, nor look on sin; therefore, when He made that blessed One "sin for us," He hid His face from Him; He forsook Him. The cross teaches the *holiness* of God with a clearness and fulness which neither the flood nor the overthrow of Sodom could do, and that because of the sinlessness of the Person Who suffered; His absolute purity, while under the imputation of sin, made Him " an offering and a sacrifice (or victim) to God for a *sweet-smelling* savour."

Having sin imputed to Him, the inflexible, un-compromising justice of God took action against Him, judged and condemned Him—condemned sin in the flesh, that the believing sinner might justly be freed from guilt and condemnation, and fully accepted in the beloved One Who died. The cross, then, teaches the *justice* of God; and in the death of Christ for sinners it proclaims the truth of the sentence of God against sin : " The soul that sinneth it shall die." Moreover, this wondrous plan of salvation, alike honourable to God and safe for the sinner who receives it, displays His *wisdom;* in a word, the cross reveals God.

If it reveals God, and teaches us what He is, so also it manifests man, proving what is in him.

Man's blindness, enmity, and guilt, were all fully proved by the rejection of Christ, and by His death on the cross; and they still are proved by the rejection of the Gospel.

If what has been said of the action of God towards Jesus, the Son of God, be true, as it unquestionably is, so also the Holy Ghost teaches us lessons of heavenly wisdom by Him who endured the cross. He instructs us in the path of perfect lowliness, patience, and love.

In Philippians ii. we have our lesson of *lowliness* taught by the humiliation of Christ, in His voluntary, and, to us, immeasurable stoop from equality with God to death, the death of the cross. Nothing is here said of advantage to us as *sinners;* it is not a question of salvation, but the presentation of a pattern mind, a perfect example of lowliness: " Let this mind be in you which was also *in* Christ Jesus," and which displayed itself by the cross.

Our lesson of *patience* is read out to us in the Gospel narrative of His steadfast endurance of the contradiction of sinners (Gentile and Jew), in His trial, mockery, and shame. He patiently endured the cross; He reviled not the reviler, nor threatened the insolent, but committed Himself to Him who judgeth righteously (Heb. xii. 2, 3; 1 Peter ii. 23). He did say, " If I have spoken evil, bear witness of the evil: but if *well*, why smitest thou Me?" But He did not say, " God shall smite thee, thou whited wall." This, His patience, is our perfect pattern.   Let us seek by grace to reproduce it in our daily life.

And what of the lesson of *love* taught us by the cross of Christ?   Oh, fellow-heir of glory, the doctrine of the cross has depths for our eternal sounding!   Howsoever much our line may be lengthened, we shall never reach the bottom any more than we shall measure its height, its length, or its breadth; this is our joy.   There will be no end to our discoveries of His love.

But what saith the Scripture on this point?   Let us hear.   If Scripture says, "God so loved the world that He gave His Son," it also says, "Christ loved the Church, and gave Himself for it."   His love to us was and is perfect, even as John confessed it to be: "Unto Him who *loveth* us, and *washed* (bathed) us in His own blood . . . . unto Him be glory" (Revelation i. 5, 6).   This is blessed; it is lovely, attractive, and powerful; but there is another aspect of this truth, a Godward side of it; namely, the mutual love, delight, and gratification of the Father and the Son; and this we must next consider.

We have already considered the cross of Christ as providing for the sinner's need; we have now to dwell upon the fellowship of the Father and the Son together in that solemn work.

This aspect of the cross is both touching and instructive to every saved sinner.   Our first thought and appreciation of the cross is our *personal advan-*

tage by it in forgiveness and salvation. But when that is known, and the cross becomes the subject of meditation and fellowship with God, how differently is it viewed! This is one mark of the difference between the babe in Christ and the father, or even the young man. Of this Divine mutual joy and fellowship we have a beautiful illustration, if not a type, in the scene on Mount Moriah. Jehovah delighted in Abraham's prompt obedience, as evidencing his *love;* Abraham took pleasure in Isaac's obedience, as proving *his* love ; and to Isaac it must have been pleasure to please his father. Anguish of heart there must have been, but love prevailed. On Calvary also, judgment, anguish and delight found their place ; displeasure and judgment against sin, anguish, unutterable anguish, in the Son as the victim, suffering under the stroke of death, the accursed death of the cross ; and who shall undertake to describe what in this sense it cost both the Father and also the eternal Spirit, through whom He offered Himself without spot to God ? Yet with all this, there was satisfaction and delight ; not, indeed, in the suffering, either as inflicted or endured, but in the love manifested, and in the purposes of grace accomplished. The Holy Ghost took pleasure in the perfection of the offering thus presented ; and although the God of truth, holiness, and justice, Whose name is love, bruised the Son, yet as the Father He delighted in the Person and obedience of His Son ; whilst the

Son delighted in rendering obedience unto death, thus meeting the deep desires of the Father's heart, and accomplishing His holy will.

This is not mere imagination; it is the burden of the testimony of the whole Word of God.

As early as the baptism of Jesus in Jordan (Jordan means "river of judgment," and was a shadow of the cross), when coming up out of the water, the heavens opened, and the Father testified His delight in the Son, and in His typical act. This was repeated in connection with a very opposite scene at the transfiguration, when the coming kingdom was presented in its heavenly and earthly glory. This approval the Son appreciated; the knowledge, the assured understanding and belief of it, was the daily rest and delight of His soul, even as He once expressed it, when speaking of the Father: "I do always the things that please Him."

To His full knowledge of this fact He also gives expression in John x. 17, 18, when, as the Good Shepherd, He says, "Therefore doth My Father love Me, because I *lay down* My life, that I may take it again. . . . This commandment have I received of My Father." To Him, love and obedience to the commandment were inseparable, even as John testifies: "*This* is the love of God, *that we keep His commandments*" (1 John v. 3).

Again, He refers to this in John xiv. 30, 31. He had walked and talked with His disciples, and taught and wrought miracles in their presence, and

now, when the time of His death was drawing near,
He said, " Hereafter I will not talk much with
you : for the prince of this world cometh, and hath
nothing in Me. But that the world may know *that
I love the Father; and as the Father gave Me commandment,* even so I do. Arise, let us go hence."
Where ? To Gethsemane and to the cross. He
had encountered Satan as the serpent in his wiles
during the forty days' temptation in the wilderness,
and Satan found nothing in Him; He was now
about to meet him as the roaring lion, with the
" strong bulls of Bashan," the angry passions of
men stirred by the devil, the deep-seated enmity
of Jews, and the scorn and derision of Gentiles;
but Satan would find nothing of evil in Him, nor
would man draw forth anything like bitterness or
retaliation from Him. Thus He went on; and
why ? To accomplish our salvation ? Doubtless;
but, as He said, while effecting that, to prove His
love to the Father, and to obey His commandment,
by laying down His life. He laid it down ; and if
none can describe the elements of sorrow and
satisfaction known only to Him in doing so, neither
can any creature fully appreciate His delight and
joy when He took again His life. He had done
that which man in innocence could not do, much
less man in his fallen condition, and which neither
Michael nor Gabriel could accomplish, for He had
fulfilled the deep desires of the Father's love, and
had done *all* His will.

Again, who shall describe the Father's joy, only equalled by that of the Son, and of the Holy Ghost ? We can believe it, and in a very little measure understand it ; but in this Divine fellowship there will ever be secrets hidden from all creatures. Christians have joy in common, yet each has a secret fellowship with the Father and with Christ. The Son of God has a name whereby He is owned—" The Word of God," and " on His vesture and on His thigh a name written, King of kings, and Lord of lords " (Rev. xix. 16). But He also has a name which no man knows but Himself, which expresses the incommunicable secret fellowship and joy between the Father, the Spirit, and Himself. We delight that it should be so, for He is worthy.

His reward will be full, His recompense abundant, in the blessing of the Church, Israel, and the nations ; His glory will be great in God's salvation ; but the source of deepest joy to Him is, and ever will be, that He has pleased, delighted, glorified, and thus gratified His Father. " The Father loveth the Son," said He, " and I love the Father."

Such are some of the lessons taught us by the cross and its work. Let us now enquire as to its practical power on the hearts and lives of those who have come to that cross for salvation.

We might speak of its power to win the heart for God ; for " we love Him because He first loved us " (1 John iv. 19); of its constraining power to live to Christ, "The love of Christ constraineth us; because . . . one died for all . . . that they which live should henceforth live . . . unto Him" (2 Cor. v. 14, 15); of the use Paul made of it to induce the Corinthian Christians to open their hearts and purses for the poor (2 Cor. viii. 9). But there is one very definite testimony to its power in Galatians vi. 14. Here Paul is defending the ground of a sinner's justification by Christ alone, which he had so fully laid down in his Epistle to the Romans. The Galatian churches were encountering Judaizing teachers, who sought to enforce circumcision on Gentile converts as essential to salvation; and he bursts forth, with holy indignation, "God forbid that I should glory, save in the cross of our Lord Jesus Christ, by whom (or whereby) the world is crucified unto me, and I unto the world."

Thus did he in a few words (not only, nor chiefly as an apostle, but as a believer) declare himself to be separated from the world, and the world from him, by the power of the cross. He thus declares that the world—profane or religious, wise or unwise, sordid or light and vain, base or refined, whether in its own outside sphere, or as seeking to creep into the Church—the world was to him, as a crucified man, only to be turned from and avoided; and, as a consequence, he was such also to the world. May we thus learn the practical power of the doctrine of the cross of Christ, and obtain victory over the world.

THE CROSS AND THE GLORY.

In reviewing Christ's life, we find at certain stages of His crossward path, the heavens opened and the Father acknowledged Him as His beloved Son, in Whom He was well pleased. This took place at the Jordan, on the Mount of Transfiguration, and when He said, "Father, glorify Thy name." On each occasion there was a voice from heaven, but when He came to the point when His obedience was perfected, instead of the opened heavens, there was darkness that might be felt, and, instead of a voice from heaven, there was a cry from earth, such a cry as had never been heard before—"My God, my God, why hast Thou forsaken Me?" To that cry there was no response from heaven. The answer came, at last, by an act. God raised Him from the dead, and thus proclaimed His heart's delight in that beloved Son, Who had perfected His obedience by His death upon the tree. Heaven opened to receive Him. Earth cast Him out; to the abyss He could not go. Where did He deserve to go? To what place? To the right hand of God. The throne of the heavens received Him as from the dead. And so it must be with His faithful followers. When the faithful witness Stephen was being persecuted unto death, he said, "I see the heavens open, and the Son of Man standing at the right hand of God." He had risen to minister to His faithful servant, and to receive his spirit. He came down to one who was suffering banishment in Patmos for His sake, to minister and to open heaven to him. So Paul tells us. " As the sufferings of Christ abound in us, so our consolation also aboundeth by Christ " (2 Cor. i. 5). He measures out His consolation according to the sorrow. God always seeks to have His gifts appreciated, and therefore it is that the supply is oft withheld till the fitting moment when we are prepared to value it. When John fell at the feet of his glorified Lord as one dead, His right hand was laid upon his head, and he heard the precious words, " Fear not." These words are never spoken except when needed; they mean too much, cost too much, to be wasted. Beloved, never shrink from a trial, never compromise to escape a trial, for in missing a trial you lose a blessing. The cross is the way to the glory, and all authority is in the pierced hand of Him who, by dying, spoiled death, and established the title to bring all who trust His precious Name to that glory which He will share with us by-and-bye.

THE POWER OF THE CROSS.

There was in the Cross and Resurrection of Christ the union of weakness and power, the weakness of death, and humiliation of the Son of God made flesh for us, but the perfect manifestation of Almighty power (2 Cor. xiii. 4). The word in 2 Cor. xii. 9, shows the normal condition of every child of God to be a like union of weakness

and power ; and if the Cross preceded the manifestation of power, the weakening of what we
imagine to be strength, must precede the demonstration of the power of God in us.

What is it that will most effectually and honourably bring down our vain thoughts as to our
wisdom and powers ? Scripture examples prove
that it is a result of nearness to God—the conscious presence of God. *There* is the light which
searches us ; *there* we get fellowship with God, Who
loves us as He searches us ; *there* our strength
is withered up. The perfect wisdom of God dis-
covers and withers up the sinews of imagined
strength and wisdom in us, and this makes us
ready for the exercise and demonstration of the
power that lifted Christ from the dust of death
and put Him on the throne of God on high.
He, as our Father, will bring us low. He will also
give us power to maintain our grasp of His love, and
power of His Spirit to lift us and make us strong.

In 2 Cor. xii. 8, 9, the thorn was that which
Paul would have least chosen, which touched him
to the quick, so that he could ask the Lord thrice
to take it from him. Thus the Lord asked thrice
that if possible the cup might pass. Both got the
same answer : *Strength*—the one to take the cup
and drain it, and come into resurrection joy ; the
other to glory in infirmities. Let us, then, glory in
the very thing that tries us most, that the power
of Christ Himself may rest upon us.

The One Offering.

IF it is necessary that believers should have right, *i.e.* Scriptural, thoughts concerning God's love, so it is also essential to the abiding peace of their souls that they perceive and believe the perfection of Christ's one offering on the cross. This is surely proved by the frequency, simplicity, and fulness with which the Holy Ghost presents it to us in the Word of God. He has pointed to it by type, from the offering of Abel down to the last offering before the cross. The same Holy Ghost now dwells in us to instruct us in the value and perfection of Christ's one offering, the antitype of all those types.

Nothing short of perfection could satisfy God, and until believers see Christ's perfectness as their's through believing, they cannot have settled peace and rest. This said, let us examine the twofold testimony of the Spirit of God; first *by* types, second *to* the antitype.

The term type (from *Túpós*, a blow, an impression, a counterpart) is something very definite. It is more than an illustration, and implies a design on the part of God to foreshadow or represent something else; and we know that by the offerings

C

under the law, *i.e.*, the old dispensation, He
designed to foreshadow the one offering of His
Son made flesh, in its varied virtues and comprehensive value.

With respect to the types, we observe a Divine
order. From the first recorded offering—that of
Abel—until the times of Moses, we read only of
one kind of offering, viz., the burnt offering—
ascending offering.

It is said of Jacob, indeed, that he offered sacrifices (Gen. xlvi. 1); but while there was plurality,
there is no mention of variety. To the eye of
God, and in His estimation, the one offering
comprehended all; and to every true believer,
whatever may have been the measure of his
intelligence, Jehovah imputed the full value of the
antitypical offering of Christ. *Now* also the babe
in knowledge has the full value of His one offering:
and the father can have no more, although he has
fuller intelligence of its value, and consequently
fuller, deeper joy in God.

The law was given by Moses, and it entered
that the offence might abound. It revealed and
defined sin as it had not before been revealed, and
to meet that revelation the variety of sacrifices
and offerings was introduced in Leviticus. As
was the revelation of sin, so also was that of the
varied virtues of the offering—burnt offering, sin
offering, trespass offering, meat and peace offerings, &c.

To us, that ritual is only a matter of history; we have nothing to do with it, thanks be to God, except by the shadow to learn more of the substance. Ours is the happy privilege of simple confidence in the one all-comprehensive offering of Christ; so that, by one glance of faith at Christ, we see all, and by presenting Him to God we present all.

The mummery of modern Ritualism is mimicry of Judaism, without the sanction from God which Judaism originally had—this is its folly; while parts of it contradict the Word of God and dishonour the sacrifice of Christ—this is its enormity, its wickedness. Beware of it, beloved fellow-believer; it betrays ignorance of dispensational differences, and also of the falseness of the idea of a state religion or a national church.

God is a Spirit, and they who worship Him must do so in Spirit and in truth ; not here only nor there alone, but everywhere. We may well be thankful to assemble within walls under cover and at set times; still, even when so gathered, if we worship aright, it is as being by faith and in spirit in the heavenlies, in the heavenly courts, where, indeed, the great High Priest, the only Priest over His brethren, leads Divine worship. This we could do, if necessary, and with equal acceptance in the sight of God, in the open field.

We have seen that by the typical sacrifices and offerings the Holy Ghost pointed to the "one

offering" of Christ in its different aspects and
results. These had their day; but we hear one
saying, in the spirit of prophecy by David,
" Sacrifice and offering Thou didst not desire ; mine
ears hast Thou opened" (or digged): " burnt
offering and sin offering hast Thou not required.
Then said I, Lo, I come: in the volume of the
Book it is written of Me, I delight to do Thy will."
This very Scripture is quoted by the Holy Ghost,
and applied to Christ on purpose to prove the
excellence of His sacrifice for sin. There is this
important and explanatory change made in this
passage. Instead of, " Mine ears hast Thou
opened," it is, " A body hast Thou prepared me."
It was by the offering of the body of Jesus Christ
once (once for all) that the mighty deed was
effected. He came to do the will of God; He
delighted to do it; it was His meat. That *will*
required that "He should lay down His life, and
take *it* again." " By the which will we are sanctified
through the offering of the body of Jesus Christ
once." See then, dear fellow-Christian, that as by
faith you are linked to that one offering which
accomplished the will of God, and reconciled you
to Him, you *are* sanctified (Heb. x. 10).

Again, in verses 11-15, He contrasts the posture
and action of the typical priests and Christ. They
stood daily ministering and *repeating* their sacrifice,
because imperfect ; but Christ, when He had made
one sacrifice for sin, *sat* down, not needing to rise

again for the purpose of offering for sin; "for by
His one offering He hath *perfected* for ever them
that are sanctified;" the one offering both sanctified
and perfected for ever, every one who is by faith
connected with it. In Ephesians v. 2, Paul, taught
by the Holy Ghost, says, "Christ also hath loved us,
and hath given Himself for us an offering and a sacrifice (victim) to God for a sweet-smelling savour."
Yes, beloved, whatever (to speak as men) that
sacrifice involved of cost, pain, and sorrow, it was,
and is, gratifying to God, and we are accepted in
Him; and that offering, in its virtue, savour, and
value, is imputed to, and reckoned to the account
of, the one who trusts it, although his faith may be
the weakest, and his intelligence of its value the
smallest.

Of old the offerer and the offering were accepted
together—it *for* him, and he *in* it; so now the
truster in Christ, and Christ the trusted One, are
accepted together. "He hath made us accepted in
the Beloved," who gave Himself *for* us. God, by
one act, has eternally accepted you in Him, in
Christ; for He changeth not. Of His gift of
Christ for us, and His calling of us to Christ, He
will not repent. In both these acts He is "without
repentance" (a change of mind). Here, then,
beloved, rest, and keep your daily Sabbath with
God by faith in His Son, and in His accomplished
work. And should you fail in your walk, should
sin defile your conscience, and so disturb your rest

of soul, the remedy is at hand. Confess fully,
definitely, believingly, and you will find the Comforter ready to fulfil His ministry, viz., the repeated
presentation to your soul of Christ in that offering
which once for all covered all your sins, and
answers fully for you in the presence of the Father.
"Little children, sin not; and if any man sin, we
have an Advocate with the Father, Jesus Christ
the righteous." For "if we confess our sins, He is
faithful and just to forgive us our sins, and to
cleanse us from all unrighteousness." Jealously
watch that nothing comes between your soul and
this, between you and Christ, but Christ only
between your soul and God. No, nothing: not
your obedience, any more than your sin. Obedience
may be—indeed, should be—the *purpose* of your life,
but not the *rest* of your soul.

Make His one offering also your shield against
the fiery darts of Satan; present Christ to him,
direct him to Christ respecting you; that is, refer
him with his every charge to Christ. If it is true,
Christ is your shield; if false, He will refute it,
and give you peace. Thus live your life as he
lived his who said, "The life that I live in the
flesh" (the body) "I live by the faith of the Son of
God, who loved me, and gave Himself for me;" in
a word, make Christ your all.

Atonement and Forgiveness.

WHAT thoughtful person does not know that, as the result of unwisely feeding and nursing infants, disease and deformity are to be found? If this is true in nature, it is equally true, and of even more importance, in things spiritual, even as the soul is of more importance than the body.

The food of newborn souls is that same Word of God by means of which they were regenerated by the Holy Ghost; it is also the guide of their steps. Consequently, to feed aright, is to feed on that Word, and to walk aright (that is, to behave correctly) is to act in obedience to it (2 Tim. iii. 16, 17).

All Scripture is essential; there is nothing in the Word of God unimportant; everything written is essential to the end for which it was written. That which is not essential to our salvation is essential to our true knowledge of God, our communion with Him, and our full obedience.

Let me, then, entreat young Christians to acquire correct, *i.e.*, Scriptural, views of God's character, and of His ways; also early, by grace, to form godly habits of watchfulness and prayerfulness, carefulness of speech and action, and unreserved obedience to His revealed will. If this is done, we shall not have a believer praying to be reconciled to God, nor a preacher of the Gospel telling unconverted people they are forgiven.

There is a difference between atonement and forgiveness; they are connected, yet distinct. The one was effected *for* us, but without us; the other is made true *in* us.

Atonement was made by Jesus to God on the cross, and *for* us; *forgiveness* is the act of God to us in Christ, and is witnessed to in our conscience by the Holy Ghost. Atonement was made before we were born; forgiveness, or remission of our sins, took place *when* we believed; we *then* "received remission of sins" (Acts x. 43; xxvi. 18).

It may be interesting and profitable to trace this difference as it appears in the Scriptures. "To the law and to the testimony" on this, as on all points.

With regard to the first; that is, "*atonement.*" It is a word which in our English translation frequently occurs in the Old Testament, but is only once used in the New (Romans v. 11), where it stands as the translation of one form of the Greek word *katallassō,* "to change, exchange, to reconcile." In the Old Testament it is the translation of the Hebrew word *kipper,* "to cover." Of this, which is its true meaning, there are many happy illustrations or examples; such as Noah *pitching* the ark with pitch, Moses making the *lid* (or *cover*) of the ark of the tabernacle, which formed the mercy-seat; but there is one very interesting use of this word which Jacob made when preparing to meet his brother Esau. Having arranged his present, he said, "I will appease" (that is, cover) "him with a present, and afterward I will see his face." As between man and man, Jacob with his present put a cover between his offence and Esau's anger, and afterward saw Esau's approving countenance.

As to the second word, "*forgiveness*," or "remission." In the New Testament these are the usual translations of the same Greek word, *aphesis.* There is another word, *apoluō*, "to loose," once used for forgiveness (Luke vi. 37); "Forgive, and ye shall be forgiven;" but both convey the idea of release, freedom from, deliverance, as we see in Luke iv. 18, where the former of these Greek words occurs in the sentence, "To preach deliverance to the captives."

This may suffice as to the Scriptural uses of the words "Atonement" and "Forgiveness." Let us now enquire as to their connection with the work of Christ.

Atonement refers to His sufferings on the cross, when He actually bore our sins and the consequent judgment of God; when He satisfied justice, expiated guilt, and paid the ransom price, in order that, by the *blood* "of His covenant, His prisoners

might be sent out of the pit in which there was
no water" (Zech. ix. 11).   In a word, when "He
through the eternal Spirit offered *Himself* without
spot to God," He performed the mighty deed of
"covering" for ever our sin and guilt, reconciling
us to God by His death, and justifying us by His
blood.   He then *atoned*, and laid the solid basis
on which God could display His grace in justly
forgiving sin; for mercy shown to the believing
sinner is an act of justice to Christ.   "The sure
mercies of David" are just and "holy things."

Forgiveness, or remission, is based on atonement.
"God for Christ's sake" (or in Christ) "hath forgiven you."   It is the act of God towards the
sinner, in virtue of his having believed in the work
of Jesus on the tree.   As a matter of experience it
stands thus: An unconverted man finds himself
convinced of sin, and discerns the fearful consequence, namely, the righteous judgment of God;
he is conscious of guilt, fearful of judgment, and
oppressed, and bound by this awful sense of God's
displeasure at his sin.   While in this state the
Holy Ghost, who has convinced him of sin, shows
him Jesus Christ, God's Son, suffering in his stead;
he believes it; the awful weight of guilt and fear is
lifted from his soul; he is free, for he has obtained
remission; the accusations of conscience give place
to the peace of God through faith in the peace-
speaking blood of Christ; the sense of God's
displeasure at his sin is exchanged for the assurance

of his acceptance in Christ, the Son of God's love; and he is happy, for he is forgiven, he is delivered. Having believed, and known the blessedness of the atonement as covering his sin, love to God takes the place of enmity, and his entire condition is changed; he is reconciled, and it is his privilege to "JOY IN GOD, through our Lord Jesus Christ, by whom he has *now received* the atonement" (reconciliation).

This is his washing or bathing (John xiii. 10), so complete that it leaves nothing to be done ever after but to wash his feet; that is, to cleanse and keep clean his daily walk through the Word.

Henceforth God is known as a Father, and with Him as such the reconciled one has to do. The severest form the dealings of God can assume towards him now is that of Fatherly correction; and, though very solemn and severe, if needs be, it is the token of Fatherly love, and the mark of his sonship, intended for his profit, to make him more holy, more like God his Father (Heb. xii. 5-11).

Even when conscious of sin, which, indeed, is too frequent an occurrence, he should have no "*conscience* of sins" (Heb. x. 2), as if the atonement had not covered all; nor should he know again his former fear of judgment and presence of guilt; but as a child he should confess his offence against a Father's love with deeper grief, and more perfect hatred of the sin than at the first, knowing that "if we confess our sins, He is *faithful* and *just* to forgive us our sins, and to cleanse us from all unrighteousness."

This childlike confession of *known* faults, together with the prayer for cleansing from secret faults (*i.e.*, faults unknown to ourselves, but seen by God), is the secret of abiding peace and joy in the Lord, and becomes power for service and suffering.

The neglect of such confession and of such prayer leads to hardness of conscience respecting sin, until God is, to speak with reverence, often obliged to give up His child to the commission of that which will put him to shame, even before men.

Israel of old opened and closed each day with the morning and evening lamb. Christ is our Lamb, whose blood once for all covered sin, and on the ground of it God, as our Father, can repeat His acts of forgiveness.

Hold fast, then, beloved, to the one sacrifice of Christ, the virtue of which is perpetual, eternal, unchangeable. By it you were reconciled to God, " reconciled by His death ; " and your position was entirely and for ever changed ; remembering this, practise without fail the confession of your faults, as a child to a father, and so walk in peace, in the light and joy of the Lord. This, I repeat, will be your strength, both for service and endurance; and you shall certainly escape the judgment of the Lord, and shame before men.

Once more, beware of false teaching on this fundamental point. The Scriptural teaching is not at-one-ment (by which is meant reconciliation *without* blood, without the cross), but atone-ment, *covering by blood*, or by the one offering of Jesus Christ on the cross. Since the fall, there is nothing for man, apart from the blood of Christ, but judgment.

Rest.

WHO but those who have tasted its sweetness can imagine the fulness and richness of that little word "*Rest?*" Let me fix it on your mind by reading a few passages in which it occurs.

Genesis ii. 3 ; Zephaniah iii. 17 ; Hebrews iv. 3-9 ; Matthew xi. 28, 29.

Our rest, which, though implied, is not distinctly stated, is God's own rest in His own blessed affections, and in the simple and absolute certainty of the accomplishment of all His works. Father, Son, and Spirit mutually delight in one another, and rest in the absolute accomplishment of every purpose which He wills to perform.

Genesis ii. 3, I need not tell you, is the rest after the six days' arrangement of matter, and the formation of man, the masterpiece of creation, and woman in man. There is a little word here we do well to notice, "He rested *from* all His works." Not from fatigue ; not that His mind needed to be refreshed through rest ; but He did all that He intended to do, and ceased. The *Sabbath Day* is always connected with the earth, and we get no mention of this Sabbath until Israel comes on the scene. There is intimation of rest in the days of Noah, when the dove was sent out of the ark, but found "*no rest*," and returned. But there is no mention of a Sabbath. It is always connected with God's dealings with the earth.

Pass on to Zephaniah iii. 17 : "He will rest *in* His love"—not *from*, as in creation. Here we have the higher, the gloriously perfect rest of redemption. God rested in His love for the object of that love : and so, dear fellow-believers, God rests in His love to you. This, of course, applies to Israel, and will have its completion by-and-bye, but the principle is the same. God has found in Christ, and in His finished work, a rest which gives Him satisfaction, and delights His heart ; and it is here you and I find rest.

"We who have believed do enter into rest." God rested from creation the seventh day ; and the Lord Jesus Christ ceased from the toil of redemption when He said, "It is finished ;" and now, sinners, hearing of the finished work of Christ, cease to work for salvation, life, and peace, and rest in it. I believe this is the first rest mentioned in the 11th chapter of Matthew. "I will give you rest ;" "Ye shall find rest to your souls ;"—a rest *given*, and a rest *found*. Some of the worst "Sabbath-breakers" are those who rigidly observe the first day of the week. Why ? Because they make observance of the first day a thread in their garment in which they seek to appear before God. We who have believed do enter into rest, and now have with God a perpetual rest in the Son of His love. There is also a perpetual Sabbath in store for the people of God.

Matthew xi. 28, 29. Sinners are not saved to do as they please. We are saved to obey the Lord, Who saved us; the standard by which we are to judge is His Word; therefore let us bring all we see around us to the test of it. We are called to take His yoke upon us, and learn of Him; that is, yoke ourselves with Him, tread the path He trod; and, lest we be in doubt as to the path He trod, the Epistle to the Philippians tells us. From the bosom of the Father, down, down to the dust of death, He Who was God, not " made Himself God," but "made Himself of no reputation." That is the yoke! coming down lower and lower in our own estimation, patiently pursuing the path He pursued. He was subject to His Father, and enjoying at that moment what He promised, "*rest*." " Take this yoke upon your neck which I am wearing, subjection to the Father; and you will find, as I do, rest to your souls."

Search out the passages in the Scriptures where the word " rest " occurs. It will richly repay you for your search. You will find that God has rested; and that Christ has rested; and that God has found for Himself, and Christ for Himself, rest; and the weary sinner coming to Christ gets rest; and the obedient son " finds rest " unto his soul. God make us more and more obedient !

Salvation.

WITH what simplicity and definiteness does the Holy Ghost in the Word present the great and glorious subject of SALVATION, and also the certain result of believing God's testimony; namely, *everlasting life*.

"He that believeth on Me *hath* everlasting life."
"He that believeth and is baptised *shall* be saved."
"He that believeth on the Son *hath* everlasting life."

Salvation is God's means to the highest possible end—His own glory. Our salvation and sonship are according to the "good pleasure of His will." God *delights* in saving sinners, and thus salvation is rendered both certain and glorious.

SALVATION PAST.

As believers, then, we *are* saved—"Who *hath* saved us, and called us." "Whom He did foreknow, He also did predestinate ; . . . whom He did predestinate, them He also called ; and whom He called, them He also justified ; and whom He justified, them He also glorified" (Rom. viii. 29-31). This is the fulness, the full scope, of God's purpose in Christ ; and it is true of *every* believer, and faith grasps it all. "Receiving the end of your faith, even the salvation of your souls" (1 Peter i. 9).

D

We *have* salvation, and praise God for it; and yet it is true that our salvation is nearer each year, each day.

To explain this, we need only consider for a moment the meaning of the word, and its varied connections in Scripture.

The meaning of salvation, as gathered from the original, both of the Old and New Testaments, is deliverance and preservation. The word is used either in a general and comprehensive sense, or in a particular and limited one.

When used in the general, it comprehends the entire work of God's grace in Christ, and Christ's perfect work, from the forgiveness of sins to the ultimate results in eternal blessing, whether to the Church of God, *i.e.*, the body of Christ, or to Israel and the nations. When employed in its limited sense, it refers to some special act of God in the economy of redemption, and the particular act may be determined by the context.

Israel's history illustrates salvation, supplying us with a faint *type* of ours, and a blessed *pledge* of theirs in the future.

The Scriptures of the Old Testament which present salvation in its entirety are abundant, such as Psalm lxviii. 20; cxlix. 4; Isaiah xlix. 6; lix. 16. In the New Testament it is presented in such passages as Acts iv. 12; xxviii. 28; Rom. x. 10; xi. 11; Titus ii. 11; Jude 3; Rev. vii. 10. These may suffice for the general application; and I pass on next to notice its *limited* application in the Word.

In Exodus xiv. 30, we read, "Thus Jehovah *saved* Israel;" and they sang, "He is become my *salvation*" (xv. 2). Here it is connected with one special act of Jehovah, by which He delivered them from Egypt, and from Pharaoh, its king; the beginning, if I may so say, of His purposed work for them.

In 1 Samuel xiv. 45, it is said, "Jonathan hath wrought this great salvation in Israel;" *i.e.*, deliverance from their enemies, the Philistines. (See also xix. 5.)

The blessed result of Jehovah's discipline of His self-willed servant Jonah was his being able to say, as a resurrection man, "Salvation is of Jehovah;" *i.e.*, salvation from the deep.

I need not multiply examples from the Old Testament, but select a few from the New.

The first of these will be found in Luke i. 68-80. (Please read the passage.) Here we have the inspired utterance of the hope of Israel based on the promises, which declared Jehovah's eternal purpose to bless them. This is a remarkable Scripture; for while it contains a description of salvation entire to *them*, no mention is made of the Church, the body, the mystery, the heavenly calling and glory, all of which are, nevertheless, included in God's salvation in Christ. The application of this passage is, therefore, *particular*, and connected with Israel.

In harmony with this were the thoughts of the apostles, and their hope before the cross, and even after the resurrection of Christ. In Luke xxiv. 21, we have their confession of this, and their great disappointment; and in Acts i. 6, their enquiry concerning the kingdom, the earthly kingdom, to Israel. The Church's standing, calling and hope had not yet been revealed; neither had the formation of the body of Christ on the earth commenced.

Such Scriptures as the above abound in the Word of God; and it would be a happy and profitable occupation to search them out, and mark their distinctive character.

I next cite that well-known, yet oft misunderstood, and therefore misinterpreted, passage, "Work out your own salvation with fear and trembling. For it is God that worketh in you both to will and to do of *His* good pleasure" (Phil. ii. 12, 13).

What a diversity of opinion has existed, and still exists, as to the meaning of this Scripture! And how much contention has a wrong and partial interpretation of it given rise to! Calvinists and Arminians, so-called, have severally contended for its meaning, whereas it bows to neither as such; for the simple truth of God is too majestic to yield to any mere system of human thought. What, then, is its teaching?

Before answering this question, I wish to remind you, my fellow-believer, that the standpoint on which the Holy Ghost places us in these particular Epistles is that of absolute possession of life—indestructible, eternal life; and that no instruction, exhortation, admonition, or warning, contained in such Epistles, can contradict, set aside, or even weaken this fact.

SALVATION PRESENT.

Remembering this, let us examine the passage in question, and we shall find that it stands in a practical connection, and is an exhortation addressed to persons already *saved*, already in Christ, and in possession of life—" To all the saints in Christ Jesus which are at Philippi " (chapter i. 1).

The Philippian believers were living in the midst of doctrinal and moral evils—among those who were slaves of the lusts, the desires of the flesh, and of the mind, and who sought to entangle them in the same. From such persons, opinions, and practices, they were to work out their salvation from day to day; their preservation, if free; and their deliverance, if entangled. Either and both these they were to effect " with fear and trembling;" distrusting their own wisdom to detect the evil, and their own strength to escape or save themselves from it; casting themselves upon Him who is the Author both of the desire and the act, whose wisdom is deeper than Satan's subtlety, and His power almighty.

Paul enumerates some of the evils by which the Philippians were surrounded, and among them that subtle but fearful sin of *selfishness*. Whether indulged in relation to things natural or spiritual, it is the bane of the "fellowship" mentioned in chapter i. 5, which is the key to the understanding of the entire Epistle. In opposition to this evil, the apostle gives the perfect example of the Son of God in His self-emptying and humiliation, even to the death of the cross, and the honour put upon Him by God in consequence (chapter ii.).

In beautiful harmony with this, Paul uses the word in his first epistle to Timothy (iv. 16), teaching him that by the faithful use of his gift, by habitual meditation, giving himself wholly to (existing, being in) the things written to him, by taking heed to himself and to the doctrine, he should both "*save* himself" and them that heard him.

In Phil. i. 19, he uses the expression again in connection with his deliverance from prison—"This shall turn to my *salvation ;*" and in 2 Tim. iv. 18, alluding to his past deliverance, and expressing his confidence in the Lord for the future, he says, "He shall deliver me from every evil work, and will preserve (*save*) me unto His heavenly kingdom."

SALVATION FUTURE.

Lastly, let us look at the word as relating to the *future*—" Now is our salvation nearer than when we believed."

It is needless for me to bring forth proof that the writer was a saved man, or that he regarded those to whom he wrote as saved ; and yet he speaks of salvation as nearing them, and that continually, even as the morning nears by so much as the night passes away.

Here, as in almost all the passages in which the Church's hope is presented, the aspect is *practical*. The words, together with those of the first part of the next verse, are inserted in parenthesis (see Greek Testament), to enforce the exhortations preceding and following.

Paul took the place of a watchman looking out for the dawn of day ; and, hailing its approach, he sought to arouse those to whom he wrote to expect it, and to order their conduct suitably to the day, awaking out of sleep, casting off the works of darkness, and putting on the armour of light.

But it may be asked, In what sense can one who is saved be said to look for salvation ?

The answer to this question will be found by considering what we are saved *to*.

We are saved *from* the judgment of God against sin. In the person of our Head and Representative, we entered the judicial court, met every charge ; in Him satisfied Divine justice, and passed out. That court is for ever closed to us, and to Him as on our account. In resurrection He was proclaimed free, and we also in Him.

We are saved from Satan's dominion, and that of the world and the flesh. We are experiencing daily preservation and deliverance, or *salvation ;* yet that very deliverance pre-supposes the existence of evil, sorrow, and pain, around us, and also our

own imperfection. But we have been apprehended
of Christ Jesus for *glory*, for resurrection perfectness
—" He hath called us to glory and virtue." We
are " predestinated to be conformed to the image
of His Son." " When we see Him we shall be like
Him." We wait, therefore, for final deliverance—
salvation from this scene of conflict and sorrow,
from the last taste and trace of our state of
humiliation and imperfection.

In virtue of our heavenly citizenship, " we look
for the Saviour, who shall change our body of
humiliation, that it may be fashioned like unto
the body of His glory." We have sonship in
Christ, the Son of God, are dwelt in by the Spirit of
sonship, and cry Abba, Father ; yet we wait for the
adoption, *i.e.*, " the redemption of our *body* "
(Rom. viii. 23). In like manner we who are saved
wait for salvation to the perfecting of our person,
condition, and place.

Then shall the Church realise her hope. Salvation shall also be brought to Israel at the revelation
of Jesus Christ ; the kingdom also shall be restored
to them (Acts i. 6 ; iii. 21), and the nations be
blessed through them.

This, our hope, will be the accomplishment of
God's eternal purpose in Christ, and the fulfilment
of promises and predictions.

Let us, then, dear fellow-believers, take this hope
and use it as our " *helmet* " (1 Thess. v. 8), and
we shall be able to lift up our head with boldness

amid the din and strife, the dust and smoke, the sorrow and trial of these evil days, holding on our way in the patience of hope.   Let us rejoice in it, and regard the passing away of time like the footfalls of Rebekah's camel, bearing her across the desert towards her unseen but beloved Isaac (Gen. xxiv. 61, 67).   Let our hearts be in advance of our steps, " looking for that blessed hope, and the glorious appearing of the great God and our Saviour," " pressing towards the mark for the prize of the high calling of God in Christ Jesus." The Lord Himself direct our hearts into the love of God, and into the patience of Christ.   Amen.

Peace.

DOUBTLESS most careful readers of God's Word have noticed the frequent recurrence in its pages of the little word "peace." Quite as much is said of it as of joy, which is the overflowing of the cup of peace. There is a joy which disturbs this peace, but there must be true peace before there can be true joy.

Peace is that which no unconverted child of Adam knows. There *is* the "triumphing of the wicked," although it is short; and there are the "pleasures of sin for *a season;*" but "there is *no* peace, saith my God, to the wicked" (Isa. lvii. 21).

The natural, unregenerate man may have health, wealth, wisdom, honour, influence, friends, comforts, a religious creed, forms and ceremonies, and may pass for a religious man; but he has no true peace; for "the way of peace have they not known" (Romans iii. 17; Isaiah lix. 8).

Yet there is, unquestionably, such a thing as true peace, and such is its nature that it is said to pass all understanding (Phil. iv. 7); it cannot, therefore, be fully comprehended; and if its possessor attempts rightly to speak of it, his soul wells up with "joy unspeakable and full of glory."

There was a time when man, fresh from his
Maker's hand, in innocence (*i.e.*, in ignorance of
evil—knowing only good), knew peace, but by disobedience he lost it; and from that moment it
ceased to be possessed by man in his natural state;
and can only be known in God's own way, through
blood, through the one all-atoning sacrifice of
Christ, God's beloved Son made flesh.

To that Sacrifice all the sacrifices of the law
pointed; and the blood shed foreshadowed the
laying down of His life for sinners on the tree,
when "He offered Himself without spot to God,"
and so "made peace by the blood of His cross"
(Colossians i. 20). Hence, God the Father, satisfied
with His Son's finished work, raised Him from the
dead, and is now known to every believer as "the
God of peace."

Here, then, we begin to treat of our subject—
peace.

PEACE WITH GOD

is the sinner's great need, and that which must be
known by him before his soul can rest. It is the
fruit of faith, not obtained by *working*, but by
believing; not by religious efforts, or resolutions to
improve a ruined condition, to amend a sinful life,
and reform conduct; but by taking the place before
God, of a guilty, ruined, helpless sinner, and
believing in the Lord Jesus Christ, trusting His
finished work, placing all confidence in Him as
made of God to every believer "wisdom, even

righteousness, sanctification, and redemption."

Should this come before the eye of an anxious soul, let me ask such an one to read carefully, as the Word of God, who cannot lie, that which He says regarding His Son in Romans iv. 25; and v. 1: "Who was delivered for (on account of) our offences, and was raised again for (on account of) our justification. Therefore being justified by faith, we have peace with God through our Lord Jesus Christ." Peace with God! This is the beginning of blessing. God reconciles to Himself in Christ, and Christ, having effected reconciliation by His death, is the true and immediate object of faith. This is *objective* reconciliation; whilst the change of mind which makes the proud, self-righteous sinner willing to be justified, saved in this way, is *subjective* reconciliation. Such a soul is at peace with God. Not as one who has *made his* peace with God, for that he never could do; but as one resting in Him, the Lord Jesus Christ, who has made peace with God *for* him, yet *without* him.

Unspeakably precious as this is, it is but the beginning of blessing; we need more than this, and God has provided more. We have rest—peace *in* God, as well as peace *with* Him. The prodigal needed food, indeed, to meet his hunger, a robe in which to cover himself, and sandals for his feet; but he had a deeper need than all these together— he needed forgiveness to relieve his conscience, for he was guilty; he needed the token of unaltered

love to satisfy his heart. The father understood
this, and ran to meet him, fell on his neck, and
kissed him, not waiting even for his confession, but
drawing it forth by the embrace and the kiss. Thus
the father relieved his own loving heart, and com-
forted his son's; and whereas other wants were
met within the house, the deeper need was met
without, and fitted the returning one to enjoy the
rich provision of the father's love. So also is it
with the sinner who believes God, and looks to, and
rests in Christ. Peace takes the place in the conscience of guilt and accusation, and love the place
of enmity, and the affections of the renewed soul
find their rest *in* God.

Reconciled to God, at peace with Him, justified
from all things, accepted in the Beloved, the saved
one possesses rest through Christ, believing in God;
for, whilst Jesus Christ, the Son of God, is the
immediate object of faith, God, even the Father,
is the ultimate rest of the soul. Through Christ
we believe in God (1 Peter i. 21), rejoice in hope
of His glory, and joy in HIM through Christ
(Rom. v. 2, 11). Thrice happy state! thrice happy
moment when it was first enjoyed!

Between that moment and the glory yet future,
there intervenes the journey here in the wilderness
and the time of service and of conflict; and it may
be asked, Is there a provision of *peace* for this also?
There is. It is possible for the believer to accomplish
his journey, perform his service, and fight his fight

in peace of heart; for the peace the Gospel gives is compared to sandals for the feet, which are included in the list of his armour as a soldier (Eph. vi. 15). In confirmation of this, let us recall the Master's words when about to leave His disciples: " These things have I spoken unto you, that in Me ye might have peace. In the world ye shall have tribulation : but be of good cheer ; I have overcome the world " (John xvi. 33). Thus, in the midst and in spite of tribulation (*i.e.*, conflict, persecution, temptation, and sorrow), it is our privilege to be in peace in Him. Neither are we left without instruction as to how it may be obtained and maintained. Turn for a moment to Phil. iv. 6, 7 : " Be careful for nothing," says Paul, " but in everything by prayer and supplication with thanksgiving let your requests be made known unto God. And the peace of God, which passeth all understanding, shall keep (garrison) your hearts and minds through Christ Jesus." Mark, dear reader, the two little words—*nothing* and *everything*. Are you tempted, persecuted, needy, straitened, sorrowful, cast down, yea, conscious even of failure in conduct ? Then pray about *all*, confess *all*. Pray definitely ; confess the particular fault, *the* thing in which you have failed or sinned ; and you will soon find your heart relieved of all, and the peace of God, God's own peace, keeping your heart and mind. Remember also Peter's words : " Casting *all* your care (anxiety) upon Him ; for He careth for (is concerned about) you."

Nor is this all; for, as the crowning blessing, God has promised to give *His* presence, His company, to be enjoyed by the obedient one, as

THE GOD OF PEACE.

In Philippians iv. 8, 9, we also have Paul's final charge: " Finally, my brethren, whatsoever things are true, whatsoever things are honest, whatsoever things are just, whatsoever things are pure, whatsoever things are lovely, whatsoever things are of good report; if there be any virtue, and if there be any praise, think on these things. Those things . . . do: and the *God of peace* shall be with you." This is the privilege of each believer, the common heritage of the children of God.

Again, this condition of soul and this manner of walk should characterize each assembly of God's people collectively. Each such assembly is comprised of individuals, and if each one walks after the heavenly pattern, God will delight to dwell among them all as the God of peace.

THE PEACE OF GOD RULING.

In Colossians iii. 15, we have the holy exhortation, " Let the peace of God rule in your hearts, to the which also ye are called in one body; and be ye thankful." Let the *peace* of God rule, direct, and be the arbiter to settle every question and arrange every matter, and let it rule in your *hearts*. The peaceful soul will sow the fruit of righteousness; that is, *peace*, and so make peace (Jas. iii. 18).

We should be ready to sacrifice any and every thing, save God's truth and a good conscience, for the peace and blessing of the whole body; so should we experience in our midst that to which we are imperatively called—peace, the peace of God—and be full of praise.

Once more, this peace is connected with the "blessed hope," the proper hope of the Church of God. The apostle Peter, when exhorting believers on the ground of the coming day of the Lord, says, "Be diligent, that ye may be found of Him in peace, without spot and blameless."

Beloved fellow-believers, let us think on these things, and seek to realize them from day to day, that, being at peace *with* God through faith in the Lord Jesus, we may rest, having peace *in* God as the portion and joy of our souls. Our hearts will then be garrisoned with the peace *of* God amid the cares, conflicts, and sorrows of the way; and we shall be so ordering our conduct from day to day that we may enjoy the presence of the God of peace, and rejoice in hope of His glory, waiting "in peace" for the coming of the Lord and our gathering together unto Him.

A Golden Chain.

W E know that the Pauline epistles are not placed in the order in which they were written. The Epistle to the Romans, first in order, was not the first Church-letter written by the apostle. But the order observed in the New Testament commends itself to the thoughtful, renewed mind as Divinely fixed; that is to say, fixed by men who acknowledged God in the arrangement of the Scriptures, and who were guided by Him.

The object of the Holy Spirit in this epistle evidently is to present, in the simplest and clearest manner, the ground on which God can and does justify the ungodly, in a way honourable to Himself and with safety to the believing sinner; namely, in virtue of the death of His Son : "being justified freely by His grace, through the redemption that is in Christ Jesus." The epistle which is first in order thus settles the first grave question between the sinner and God, even his salvation. Although this is the special point, the prominent feature, of the Epistle to the Romans, it is not the only one; but rather, from this point the Holy Spirit, by the apostle's pen, leads us on and up, step by step, to the elevation and triumph with which chapter viii. closes, and from whence Paul descends or branches off in chapters ix., x. and xi., to the national question of Israel and the Gentiles.

By these few general remarks we introduce the subject, which may be termed *"A Golden Chain; or, God's purpose of grace in Christ."* We read :— " Whom He did *foreknow*, He also did *predestinate* ; . . . . whom He did predestinate, them he also *called ;* and whom He called, them He also *justified ;* and whom He justified, them He also *glorified* (Rom. viii. 29, 30).

With God counsel precedes action, and purpose gives birth to promise and prediction : hence " calling," one link in this chain, fulfils purpose— *" called* according to His purpose." In harmony with this is the order of the Spirit's ministry in and through Christ. When Jehovah presented Him to Israel through Isaiah, He said, " The Spirit of Jehovah shall rest upon Him, the Spirit of wisdom and understanding, the Spirit of counsel and might "—counsel first, and then might ; a blessed example to us to form our plans in secret with God, and then to act ; to think under His eye before we speak.

God, then, had a purpose of grace towards us before He called us with an effectual and holy calling, " not according to our works, but according to His own purpose and grace given us in Christ Jesus before the world began " (2 Tim. i. 9). And

in the passage from Rom. viii., cited above, we
have the five links of this chain, which begin and
end with God Himself. This order is ever true of
all that emanates from God—"*Of* Him, and *through*
Him, and *to* Him, are all things;" therefore, "to
Him be the glory for ever."

In considering this subject, we will follow the
order observed by the Holy Spirit, and commence
with—

1.—FOREKNOWLEDGE.

" Whom He did *foreknow*." The foreknowledge
of God is declared by Himself, witnessed to by
others, and proved by events. In Isaiah we find
Jehovah repeatedly challenging idolators and idols
on this ground ; see chapters xli. 22, 23 ; xlvi. 10 ;
and xlviii. 3-9. When instructing Jeremiah in his
service as a prophet, He said, " Before I formed
thee I *knew* thee " (chap. i., 5). In Acts iv., 28, we
find the assembly of believers testifying to God's
foreknowledge ; and the facts referred to prove it.
" Known unto God are all His works from the
foundation of the world." Nothing that happens
increases His knowledge or surprises Him, however
new it may be to us. " He calleth things that be
not, as though they were."

But what did God foreknow concerning these
believers at Rome, and therefore concerning us ?
He foreknew their coming into being, time, place,
and parentage; but did He foreknow or foresee any

moral excellence, any good thing, anything better in them or in us than in others ?   Certainly not ; all are alike born in sin and shapen in iniquity ; there is "no difference" in this respect.   All distinctions between man and man are outward and circumstantial, and before God *all*, in virtue of their descent from Adam, are sinners; and, as a fact, the saved are often the most unlikely by nature to be so.   They were foreknown as those fitted for that exhibition of sovereign grace which is His glory ; and in the wisdom of God, only wise, they were "*predestinated*," according to the purpose of Him who worketh all things after the counsel of His own will.

2.—PREDESTINATION.

Here again we have to enquire, What is predestination ?   The word occurs several times in the New Testament ; it is, therefore, important that we should know its meaning.   The English word "predestinate" is simply to decree or determine beforehand : and the Greek word used here is similar—"to fix determinately, to decree, to destine beforehand" (see Acts iv. 28.)

God, then, foreknew us as ruined in the first Adam and bearing his fallen image (1 Cor. xv. 49), and as therefore just suited to the display of His grace in Christ Jesus, the last Adam ; He chose us in Him before the foundation of the world; definitely fixed or predestinated us in Christ *unto sonship* (Eph. i. 4, 5), "to be conformed to the image of His Son" (Rom. viii. 29), that He might, in resurrection, be "the Firstborn among many brethren," all by grace bearing the likeness of Him who is essentially the "image of the invisible God."

Such was His purpose in Christ Jesus before time, and on the ground of this purpose He began to act on sinners at Rome in the apostles' day, and since then on us. Finding us in sin's darkness and death, "alienated from the life of God," He "*called*" us.

3.—CALLING.

This is the third and centre link in this golden chain, and until we were brought under its power we had no warrant to trace the other links, either backward or forward ; but now we can do so with joy. What is it, then, to be "called ?" Other Scriptures refer to God's call. Paul acknowledges these very Christians in Rome as among "the *called* of Jesus Christ." Of himself he wrote to the Galatians, "When it pleased God, who separated me (like Jeremiah) from my mother's womb, and *called* me by His grace, to reveal His Son in me ;" and when he was defending the truth of God before the Galatians he expressed his astonishment that they were so soon removed from Him who "called" them in the grace of Christ. Is *calling*, then, the presentation of the Gospel and the commandment to believe in it ? It is surely

far more than this; for observe, that those who are
called are justified—"Whom He *called*, them He
also justified." But all who hear the Gospel and
the command to believe it are not justified; therefore, calling is something more than the outward
hearing of the Gospel. Yes, beloved fellow-
Christian, you and I know that it is nothing less
than the sovereign act of God's mercy in regener-
ating the soul by His Spirit and His word: "As
many as received Him . . . were *born of God*"
(John i. 12, 13). "Of *His own will* begat He us
with the word of truth" (James i. 18). We know
that the proud reasonings of man's corrupt heart
rebel at this. In Paul's day human pride objected
to it, replying against God; and now that it is
more than ever rife, it should be met with the same
reproof with which Paul met it—"Who art thou,
O man, that repliest against God?"

In Adam's fall, the whole race of which he was
the head also fell, and became as the clay, the
"lump" of which Paul speaks in chapter ix. of this
epistle. All were obnoxious to the justice of God,
and if all had been left to perish, God would have
been just, for all had sinned. But it is on this
"lump" that the God of grace is pleased to act in
sovereign right of mercy, "to show His glory on
the vessels of *mercy* which He had *before prepared*
unto glory, even on us whom He hath *called*, not
of the Jews only, but also of the Gentiles."

It is sad to find the amount of opposition that

exists against this truth even among God's children, owing to the lack of full subjection to God's Word. But the fact remains. God *called* then, and calls now, and "whom He called, them He also *justified*."

4.—JUSTIFICATION.

What is it to be justified? "How shall man be just with God?" was a question raised by Job of old. The verb "to justify" in the original means "to hold as guiltless, to accept as righteous;" therefore, to be justified is to be cleared, acquitted, approved and accepted. If we are by nature guilty and condemned, and if there is to be no compromise of God's character, but the display of all His attributes—of justice equally with mercy; no lessening of the guilt of sin, nor relaxing of the sentence against it—how is this to be effected? Again, if He who has the right to condemn and the power to execute the sentence, is the One who clears and accepts, we still have to ask and discover *how*. The answer is given in the infallible Word of God.

We have seen that it is "God that justifieth" (Rom. viii. 33); "The Scripture, foreseeing that God would justify the Gentiles through faith" (Gal. iii. 8); again, "that He might be just, and the justifier of him which believeth" (Rom. iii. 26). This He does in grace. Man has no claim on Him for justification; he deserves nothing but judgment; he is a sinner, declared by God to be such, and nothing else (Gen. vi. 5); his conduct without an exception proves it, for "there is none that doeth good, no, not one" (Rom. iii. 12); and when convinced by the Holy Spirit of his real state he confesses it to be so. Therefore, justification must be by grace, by free favour; and so it is written, " being justified *freely* by His grace " (Rom. iii. 24). Christ's finished work is the ground on which a righteous God, whose name is Holy, can honourably acquit all who believe on Christ Jesus. In Him we are justified—"justified by His *blood*," not by His life; but being reconciled by His death, we are also " saved by His life." By virtue of Christ's endless life, with all its activities and capabilities, we are preserved to the end, to eternity; for He has said, " Because I live, ye shall live also." Faith enables our souls to apprehend the value of His justifying blood, and unites us to the living Christ of God, so that we are "justified by faith ;" and the faith by which we are thus justified " without works," produces good works; and, therefore, as James teaches, we are also "justified by works."

What grace of God, to pardon and accept in the Son of His love everyone who rests in Him, and in His finished work! What more could He do? Yet one thing more, which forms the last link in this chain: "Whom He justified, them He also *glorified*."

5.—GLORY.

In answer to the prayer of the Lord Jesus in

John xvii. 1, God has glorified His Son (Acts iii. 13), taking Him up from the dust of death, into which He had brought Him for our sakes, receiving Him up into heaven, and seating Him at His own right hand in the heavenlies, "far above all principality and power and might and dominion, and every name that is named, not only in this age, but also in that which is to come," the age of millennial glory. God "raised Him up from the dead and gave Him glory," and in Him, the members of His body, the Church, have been raised up also, and made to sit together with Him in the heavenlies, so that, virtually, we have been "glorified." Yes, God who reached us by the wondrous stoop of His beloved Son unto death, has uplifted us by His power through the cross, and has brought us to HIMSELF, to participate in the glory He has given to Christ; and that glory will yet be manifested, for "when Christ, who is our life, shall be manifested, then shall ye also be manifested with Him in glory."

God's foreknowledge and predestination of us were before time; we have experienced this calling in time, and give God thanks. On the testimony of His word we rest, assured that we *are* justified by His grace through faith, and we rejoice; but for the last link—our manifestation in glory—we hope, and are called patiently to wait. "When He shall be manifested we shall be like Him," and shall be glorified together with Him.

Thus, beloved fellow-saints, we see that God

has, for His own eternal glory, and our eternal joy, bound us to Himself by this golden chain of inseparable links; and may the knowledge and belief of this move us to diligence, to constant, simple trust, and to whole-hearted devotedness in service, and also enable us joyfully to endure whatever suffering He is pleased to lead us through. To Him be glory. Amen.

Divine Love.

WHO is sufficient to treat this mighty subject —the power of love? Surely none can do so with a thought of accomplishing more than an attempt to set it forth! "God only knows the love of God," yet would we delight to speak of it, and seek to know it more perfectly, admire it, and worship.

There are four little words often repeated in the New Testament—love, grace, mercy, and peace. All these are true in Him, yet each differs from the others.

LOVE is the nature of God; for we read, "God is Love." He is the self-supplied source of all blessing—of rest, joy, and delight. The manifestation of love is the revelation of God; it is the source of all the rest—" God *so* loved that He *gave*."

GRACE is the manifestation of favour to the undeserving, not looking for merit in its object. It is the free favour of God. Everything better than the worm that never dies, and the unquenchable fire, is a favour from God, and could only be bestowed through the cross; and it is this grace of God that bringeth salvation from these. "It is of *faith*, that it might be by *grace*," and therefore *sure* to all who receive it.

MERCY points to the real condition of its object as being miserable, out of which state mercy raises it, delivering from misery.

PEACE describes the state to which God, in His grace and mercy, raises the objects of His love, viz., reconciliation *to*, and rest *in*, Himself.

Divine love, ever true in God, is true in all who believe—they love. " We love Him, because He first loved us." " We have known and believed the love that God hath to us " (1 John iv. 16). " God is love," and of Him, of His love, we long to know more and more.

With this desire to know more of that love which passeth knowledge, let us enquire what He has effected—what is the *power* of love ?

The God of love purposed from eternity to reveal His love, *i.e.*, Himself; and, in the foreknowledge of the creature's ruin by sin, determined to bring in redemption, and that through the gift of His Son. In due time He sent Him, giving His Son for the salvation of every one who believes, " that whosoever believeth in Him should not perish, but have everlasting life." Having given Him, He did not spare Him from death, but "delivered Him up for *us* all." Thus wrote a believing man, an apostle, to his fellow-believers, " for *us* all."

The Son of God loved in fellowship with the Father, and gave Himself for the Church, redeeming it by Himself, to Himself, and to the Father. Such was the mighty achievement of Divine love, unequalled love.

Beloved reader, we desire to fix your thoughts and faith on this precious subject, leaving you to trace it downward to the simplest token and display of its power. This gift insures every other good; this victory, obtained by love upon the cross, pledges every other true deliverance. It is the unanswerable argument for God against every enemy, and should silence the clamour of unbelief. God *so* loved that He gave His Son; hence the exulting exclamation, "How shall He not with Him also freely give us all things?"

This love of God, beloved fellow-Christian, is, indeed, an ocean vast, without bottom, without shore, free from rocks, from shoals, and reaches— in which we may swim, dive, and take our heavenly pastime without fear. This love of God is our rest, our delight. *In this*, and *by it in us*, we shall " have boldness in the day of judgment : because as He (God) is, so are we in this world" (1 John iv. 17).

This love, moreover, in its manifestation, is our pattern, as He said who manifested it perfectly, " that ye should love one another, *as* I have loved you." If He laid down His life for us, we ought also to lay down our lives for the brethren. " Walk in love, as Christ also hath loved us, and hath given Himself for us " (Eph. v. 2).

Of the power of this love in us, in men of like

passions with ourselves, we have many striking examples in the Word of God (both in the Old Testament and in the New), in Israel, and in the Church of God. Brevity forbids our enumerating many illustrations; indeed, it is not necessary. One specially bright example of love as a mighty incentive stands on record in the Old Testament— one often referred to, oftener, perhaps, than imitated in principle. I mean the loving, loyal deed of David's three mighty men, who, on hearing him express his longing for water from the well of Bethlehem, jeopardized their lives, and brought it him. They did, indeed, surrender their lives for him, and he so regarded their conduct; for he would not drink the water, but poured it out before Jehovah, saying, " Shall I drink the blood of these men ? " And further to prove his estimate of their service, he placed them first in honour ; they ranked first among his mighty men; others were promoted, but none attained to *their* rank.

Many are the recorded acts of daring courage performed, advantages surrendered, and sufferings endured, all proceeding from love ; love prompted and sustained, and in the service found its reward.

In the New Testament also many bright exemplifications of the power of love might be singled out. Peter loved much and ardently, and at the end of his course proved it, enduring a measure of suffering, which he avowed himself ready for even before he was called to it, suffering ultimately unto death.

John also, if he did not lay down his life as a martyr for Christ, laid it out (and that a long one) in patient service and suffering for His name—a severer trial, perhaps, than that of death. These were bright examples; but for combination of character, conduct, ministry, and service, we judge Paul to have been the first, and nearest that of the blessed Master, manifested in his elevation as to truth, with lowliness of mind and meekness of spirit; in his tender bowels, prayers and tears for Israel, with uncompromising boldness in the truth against their unbelief; in his deep, tender, nurse-like care for the saints, even for the weakest, with unflinching faithfulness in reproving their faults, even those of an apostle—love which led him to say, " Most gladly will I spend and be spent for you ; notwithstanding the more abundantly I love you, the less I be loved ;" which also enabled him to say, " I kept back nothing that was profitable unto you. . . . I declared unto you the whole counsel of God ;" and again, without hypocrisy, to testify, " If I be offered (poured out) upon the sacrifice and service of your faith, I joy, and rejoice with you all." Yet he spared not either false doctrine or practice, nor overlooked their wrong thoughts or ways.

Such as these were prominent witnesses to the power of divine love *in* them, and doubtless the day of Christ will reveal many examples which have been hidden from the eyes of man. Our David, our

Beloved, sees all such faithful workers, estimates duly, and will openly declare in that day His value of and delight in them.

We know a little of that which love has effected *for* us, and are desirous of knowing it more fully, and believing it more simply. We also know somewhat of the power of divine love *in* us, and we pray that it may increase more and more. Let us, then, as a means to that end, contemplate oftener than hitherto His love to us, and believe it more confidently; so shall our love increase and abound, and manifest itself in a more Christ-like walk in the midst of our fellow-saints, and before the unsaved world around us.

Blessed be God, there *are*, even in our day—a day of weakness, worldliness, and division—many fair witnesses to this great truth, the love of God, who with simplicity of mind believe it, and in their lives exemplify its power. Let us, then, endeavour more earnestly than ever to "forget those things which are behind, and reaching forth unto those things which are before, press toward the mark for the prize of the high calling of God in Christ Jesus."

Sanctification.

NOT many words are in more general use at the present time in the comparatively enlightened parts of Christendom than "*Sanctification*" and "*Perfection;*" yet notwithstanding the clearness with which some perceive and declare their meaning, there is still much indistinctness in apprehending and inaccuracy in stating their true import.

In many such cases, perhaps in most, the difficulty lies in a misapprehension of what the *flesh* is; *i.e.* our corrupt nature, derived from our union with the first Adam, with which we were born, and thereby constituted sinners before we were manifestly such by evil words and deeds. "Behold, I was *shapen* in iniquity; and in sin did my mother *conceive* me," said David, when he had learned in the presence of God the utter depravity of his very nature (Psalm li. 5).

In this evil nature we lived, and to it we were slaves, until God, in His rich, sovereign, mighty grace, delivered us by a birth from above, through faith in the Lord Jesus Christ. From that time we ceased to be "*in* the flesh," and were, and still are, "*in* the Spirit," and indwelt by the Spirit of Christ.

But although we are no longer in the flesh, the

F

flesh is still in us, and it "lusteth against the Spirit;" hence the inward conflict from day to day. The corrupt root remains unchanged. Though life from Christ has been communicated to us, and we are a new creation after the image of Him who created us, no change is effected in the character of the flesh. Our Lord's words to Nicodemus, who was a cultivated man as to the flesh, are still true, " That which is born of the flesh *is* flesh," even as " that which is born of the Spirit *is* spirit." Therefore, sanctification is neither the eradication or out-rooting of the flesh, nor even an improvement in its nature.

Experience within and observation of facts around, combine to confirm this statement, and prove that "the old man" will struggle to the end.

What, then, is sanctification? To this inquiry, I purpose to reply by examining some of those Scriptures in which the word occurs, and others by which the idea underlying it is most clearly conveyed.

Let us take the first mention of this subject, in Gen. ii. 3 : " And God blessed the seventh day, and *sanctified* it : because that in it he had rested from all His work which God [Elohim] created and made." Observe, no mention is made of any difference between this day and the other six as to its length, its light, or heat, but only as to its particular use ; it was separated, set apart by God to Himself, for a purpose, even *rest*. Here we have the true meaning of the term " sanctification," *a setting apart*.

Again, it is said, in Lev. viii. 10, that Moses "sanctified" the tabernacle, and all that was therein. Not that he changed the nature of gold, silver, copper, and wood, nor of linen and silk, or other materials of which the tabernacle had been constructed, or with which it was furnished; but he separated them from common purposes, to Jehovah's use, for His worship by Israel. The same applies to persons; for Moses afterwards consecrated Aaron and his sons, to sanctify them to the priestly office and its functions. (See *vv.*12,30.)

For brevity's sake, I will only cite one more passage in which the word "sanctify" occurs, and that in a remarkable connection, but not less clearly presenting its true meaning; if possible, more so. In Isaiah lxvi. 17, we have these striking words : " They that *sanctify* themselves, and purify themselves in the gardens behind one tree in the midst, eating swine's flesh, and the abomination, and the mouse, shall be consumed together, saith Jehovah." Here are men who separate themselves from temple, altar, and priest, defiling themselves with abominable creatures, yet they are said to "sanctify themselves;" *i.e.*,they *separate* themselves to evil, and meet with the just recompense of their conduct.

I will now ask the reader to examine at his leisure the many passages in which this word is found, and the result will be the confirmation of what has been stated. I might add that lexicographers give the same meaning to the term. Parkhurst says, in his article on the Hebrew word, " To separate, to set apart." That *separation* or *setting apart* is the ideal meaning of the word, appears from Leviticus xx. 24, compared with verse 25, " I have separated you from other people ; " " Ye shall not make your souls abominable by beast or by fowl, or by any manner of living thing that creepeth on the ground, which I have separated from you as unclean ; " the animals thus separated remaining, of course, unchanged and as unclean as before. Dr. Young gives a similar explanation of the word.

Having gathered thus much from the Old Testament Scriptures, let us now examine some from the New, in which the corresponding Greek word is employed, both in the Gospels and Epistles. Here also the idea throughout is separation, or setting apart.

In proof of this, notice first those remarkable words uttered by our blessed Lord in connection with the Father. In answer to the cavilling Jews, who objected to His calling Himself the Son of God, and who founded thereon the charge of blasphemy, He said, " Say ye of Him, whom the Father hath *sanctified*, and sent into the world, Thou blasphemest ? " (John x. 36.) This cannot mean that the Father made Him pure or holy, for He was so essentially and eternally as the Son and Word of God, and also in incarnation ; but it tells us that the Father set Him apart for the work which He came to accomplish.

Again, in John xvii. 19, He says, "And for their sakes I *sanctify* myself, that they also might be sanctified through the truth." Here we have the same idea expressed—not His making Himself holy, but separating or setting Himself apart as the Offering without spot to God, in virtue of which the Father constituted Him, in resurrection, "a priest for ever after the order of Melchisedec;" for He glorified not Himself, nor set Himself apart to be a high priest.

Space forbids enlarging on this part of the subject. Let us now enquire the force of the term as applied to ourselves. That there is such a thing as sanctification we are sure; we know it is the will of God that we should be holy. Our Lord's prayer was, "Sanctify them through Thy truth;" and Paul also prayed that believers might be sanctified wholly, spirit, soul, and body, and might be preserved blameless (1 Thess. v. 23). In what, then, does our sanctification consist? It is neither more nor less than the subjugation of the flesh, the corrupt nature derived from our Adam-standing, by the power of the Holy Ghost, who dwells in us, in order that the new life may be manifested, that the principles of the new creation may be developed, and that we may reflect the moral glory of Christ; walking in the Spirit, walking even as He walked.

Sanctification is connected in the Word of God with each person of the Godhead; but the Father,

Son, and Holy Spirit are always one in counsel, and united in action—a blessed pattern of all fellowship in the truth, and co-operation in service.

Jude, in his epistle, addresses the believers as " sanctified by God the Father, preserved in Jesus Christ, and called." In the Epistle to the Hebrews we read, " Jesus, that He might sanctify the people with His own blood, suffered without the gate " (chap. xiii. 12) ; sanctifying Himself that they might be truly sanctified. Peter, in his first Epistle (chapter i. 2), says, " Elect according to the fore-knowledge of God the Father, through [or in] sanctification of the Spirit, unto obedience and sprinkling of the blood of Jesus Christ." Again, in that unique passage in which Paul describes his service and the fruit of his labours among the Gentiles, he speaks of the saved ones among them and their service as being an acceptable priestly offering, or presentation to God, " sanctified by the Holy Ghost " (Rom. xv. 16).

Thus we see that believers were sanctified by God, set apart, chosen in Christ, before time ; that in time they were sanctified by the blood, by that one Offering which both sanctifies and perfects for ever ; that in their day they are sanctified by the Holy Ghost in regeneration and belief of the truth, sanctified by the Word.

Sanctification by the Holy Spirit in regeneration is instantaneous, though its development and its manifestation may be gradual and progressive.

The moment life is communicated to anyone from Christ, the Head and Source, that moment he is separated from the world, delivered from death and darkness. Subsequent practical separation from sin, and devotedness to God, are the manifest result; so that, while "progressive sanctification" is not a Scriptural term, growth in grace and knowledge of Christ is a reality which is revealed, commanded, and by grace effected.

In all this the flesh remains the same, precisely what it was—conquered, but not changed. No amount of knowledge or power of grace, no height of joy or depth of sorrow, can either outroot or change it. Neither Gethsemane nor Tabor would improve it; nor could Paul's marvellous introduction to the third heavens destroy it; for he needed a thorn in the flesh when he came down from the third heavens to preserve him from the pride of his nature, which would otherwise have fed on the wonders of that heavenly region, and would have puffed him up.

Once more, as to our sanctification through the Word. "Sanctify them through Thy truth : Thy Word is the truth." The answer to this prayer is effected by the application of the Word to our spirit, words, and ways; to all that passes within and around us. By this means we discover that which is contrary to the mind and ways of Christ in either and all of these; and through the power of the Holy Spirit, who indwells us, we stand

practically free, separated from them, and avoid
that which is evil. Again, from the Word we learn
what is pleasing to God according to Christ Jesus,
and by the same power we practise it. Thus the
Word forms and fashions our life and conversation
as the mould does the clay; as it is written, "Ye
have obeyed from the heart that form of doctrine
to which ye were delivered." This is the washing
"by the Word," which He who loved the Church
and gave Himself for it is now continually carrying
on (Ephesians v. 26). Not washing the *flesh*, but
cleansing us from the power of that flesh in ourselves, and in its works around us, by the application
of the Word, and by the power of the Holy Ghost.
For what we know experimentally of this, let us
give thanks, and forgetting that which is behind of
this race, let us press forward along the line for the
goal and the prize.

In conclusion, let me say that we have no lower
standard of walk than the walk of Christ, nor can
we justify any manifestation of the flesh. There is,
indeed, forgiveness with God, but we must not find
excuses for our sins. The same apostle who says,
"We have an Advocate with the Father," and that
"if we confess our sins, He is faithful and just to
forgive us our sins," says also, "My little children,
these things write I unto you, that ye *sin not*."

The Holy Spirit is of almighty power to subdue
the flesh, and our aim should be *full* obedience to
the will of God, as revealed in His Word.

Perfection.

THIS subject is intimately connected with that of the former paper— Sanctification, or Holiness—and calls for similar examination and test by Scripture.

Perfection characterizes every work of God, His Word and His ways. It distinguishes the person and work of the Lord Jesus, and also the Holy Spirit and His work. Nothing short of it can satisfy the children of God, or fully display the power of grace.

We are commanded by the Lord Jesus to be perfect. The apostle Paul likewise exhorts us to go on to perfection, and it is that which every believer will ultimately reach; for God's work is perfect.

In this, as in sanctification, flesh has no part; it cannot help us to attain it; on the contrary, it only hinders. In connection with such subjects we have nothing to do with the flesh, save to reject its counsel, and paralyse its action.

What, then, is perfection? For an answer to this question let us, as before, appeal to Scripture, examining some of the many passages in which " perfection " and " perfect " occur. These words are not always the translation of the same original words; for different Hebrew and Greek words, conveying different meanings, are thus rendered.

In selecting a few Scriptures from the many, we will commence with that in which the word " perfect " is first used; viz., Genesis vi. 9: " Noah was *perfect* in his generation." He was perfect (Heb., *tamim*), "plain, or complete." This he was in his generation in contrast with those who surrounded him; "for all flesh had corrupted his way on the earth." But, although perfect in his generation, Noah was not sinless; this fact his subsequent conduct proved.

The same might be said of Abraham, who was bidden to walk before the Almighty, the self-sufficing and omnipotent God, and be perfect (*tamim*); not that he was to be free from weakness and failure, but true to his knowledge of God and of sin. We doubt not but that his aim was to avoid sin and please God, yet we never hear him speak of *sinless perfection*, neither did he attain it.

The testimony borne by Jehovah to Satan respecting Job was that he was " a perfect (*tam*) and an upright (*yasher*, straight, even) man, fearing God and eschewing evil." He was perfect in intention, and upright in conduct—true to his knowledge of good and evil, but no more sinless than was Noah. Indeed, the great lesson Job had to learn by all his severe trials was, that, notwithstanding his life of integrity, of which he boasted,

he was vile in his nature, and that the only place
for him was "dust and ashes" in self-abhorrence
and repentance.

In Deut. xviii. 13, the children of Israel were
charged to be "perfect" with Jehovah their God.
Taken in its connection, perfection here means
perseverance in separation from idolatry, witch-
craft, and dealing with familiar spirits, and continu-
ance in the worship of Jehovah only. That it did
not mean sinlessness, is evident from the fact that
they were under solemn obligation to offer the
morning and evening lamb; nor could even the
priest dare to approach the altar, except he first
washed at the laver. They knew not sinless
perfection; indeed, Scripture knows it not, save in
Him who was undefiled and undefilable in Himself,
even when under the imputation of sin, and when
judged for it. Rather we should say, that if at
any one moment beyond another He was the
object of His Father's delight, it was when "He
bare our sins in His own body on the tree." To
present this sacrifice in type was a part, and a
considerable part, of Israel's *perfection* with
Jehovah their God.

In David's inspired song (2 Sam. xxii.), on the
occasion of his deliverance from Saul, and from all
his enemies, we find the expression, "I was also
upright (perfect, *tamim*) before Him." Was this
an assertion of sinlessness? We know it was not,
so far as David's flesh was concerned; yet he was

perfect in his conduct towards Saul, not injuring, but delivering him, though Saul was, without cause, his enemy, and sought his life. David's motto was, " Touch not the Lord's anointed ;" and to this he was perfect, and with the upright Jehovah showed Himself upright, and delivered him. David was conscious of uprightness, but knew too much of himself to speak of sinlessness. Doubtless the Spirit of Christ carried David beyond himself in this song to utter words of unqualified application to David's Lord.

The habit of quoting Old Testament Scriptures, describing Jehovah's work with, and in, His ancient people Israel, and applying them in an unqualified manner to ourselves, often misleads.

Space demands that we now pass on to the New Testament. Here the first occurrence of the word "perfect" is in Matt. v. 48 : " Be ye *perfect*, even as your Father which is in heaven is perfect." The subject of this passage is kindness to enemies, and the perfect example of it is seen in God's conduct ; for He causes His sun to shine, and His rain to fall on the unjust as well as on the just. To be perfect (*teleios*), complete, as taught here, is to love our enemies, and do good to those who hate us, and so to imitate God, reflecting His glory in the grace of our ways. To be kind to the thankful only, would be a coming short in our representation of Him ; it would be *imperfection.*

This conformity will not be effected by the

eradication of selfishness, nor by changing it into unselfishness, but by the subjugation of self, that the love of God in us may manifest itself after the Divine pattern. It will not be the result of the non-existence of sin in us ; it will not be sinless perfection.

The rich young man who came to Christ to enquire what he was to do to inherit eternal life, and who professed to have kept the commandments enumerated by Christ, was told that if he would be perfect (*teleios*) he must go and sell all, give to the poor and follow Christ. He could not reach that mark, he could not *complete* the course of obedience, he was not *perfect* ; nor can the natural man ever be so. As children of God, we shall complete our course in resurrection at the coming of the Lord. Then we shall reach the stature of a "*perfect* man " (Eph. iv. 13). Towards this let us press onward.

In Matt. xxi. 16, we have the word " perfected " as the translation of another Greek word (*katartizo*) : " Out of the mouth of babes and sucklings Thou hast *perfected* (fitted, thoroughly adjusted) praise ;" for praise is beautifully adapted to the lips of the saved, as their lips are fitted to sing to the glory of God.

In Luke vi. 40, we have it again : " Every one that is perfect shall be as his Master ;" or, " Every one shall be *perfected* as his Master." The Master was perfected because He was, through suffering, perfectly adapted to us as a Saviour, and the servant must be adapted to the Master by the same process. Take as an example of this the apostle Paul. When it pleased the Lord to take him up into Paradise to see sights and hear words which it was not lawful to utter, he was in danger of being puffed up and imagining himself strong, in which state of mind he would be unfitted for Christ's use, and for His purpose to exalt Himself in Paul. In order, therefore, to preserve him, there was given him a thorn in the flesh, to effect in him conscious weakness, which was exactly, beautifully fitted to the strength of Christ; for in that weakness the strength of Christ was *perfected*. On the discovery of this Paul gloried in the Divinely-chosen means to such a blessed end. It is so with us; our circumstances are wisely arranged, suited to the end of fitting us to receive and value the sympathy and power of Christ. There could be no suitability between a once suffering and still sympathetic Head, and members who knew nothing of sorrow or weakness, and there would be no occasion for the perfecting of His ability in their experience.

In Eph. iv. 11, this word is used in connection with the body of Christ. Paul states that the Lord, who descended to save, ascended to bestow gifts—apostles, prophets, evangelists, pastors and teachers —for the *perfecting* of the saints, in order to the work of the ministry, to the edifying of the body.

These were given for the perfect adjustment and fitting of the members, each in its own place to perform its own functions, that the body might be built up, edified, making increase by that which every joint supplied. In all this there is not the remotest idea of sinlessness in the members; indeed, the flesh ever hinders the happy development of this work in the saint. Perfection in this connection would be the manifestation of entire unity by means of the diversity. Alas! where shall we find it?

Writing to the Corinthian Church, a disorderly assembly, Paul, using the same word as in Eph. iv. 11, exhorts them to be "*perfectly joined* together in the same mind and the same judgment," and in like manner bids them be "perfect" and "of good comfort" (2 Cor. xiii. 11), adding, "This also we desire, even your perfection."

To the Thessalonians he wrote, "That I might *perfect* that which is lacking in your faith;" that by fuller instruction in the truth, their faith might be more fully exercised and fitted to the truth on all points. Truth and faith were to be adjusted. Sinlessness is not implied here.

Another Greek word is translated by "perfect" in Rev. iii. 2: "I have not found thy works *perfect* (filled, from *plēroō*, to make full, to fill) before God." So also Paul, writing to the Corinthians, "When your obedience is *fulfilled*." There might be obedience, but not *full* obedience; there might be

an obeying in all points known, yet not *perfect*
obedience; indeed, only of One could it be said, in
this sense, that His obedience was perfect. The
most obedient saint is never satisfied with his
measure of obedience. No one will say he is perfect,
if he makes Scripture his standard. If any can
say they are by grace upright, true to their light,
albeit they may be ignorant on some points (and
ignorance of revealed truth may be culpable), let
them not imagine that they are sinless, that the
flesh is either eradicated or changed.

Should any say they are what Paul declared he was
not, namely, *perfected* (as the word is in Phil. iii. 12),
their folly would be manifest; but if they are *perfect*
(according to verse 15), *i.e., instructed, established,*
let them prove it by forgetting the things which
are behind, and reaching forth to those things
which are before, pressing along the line to the
goal for the prize, which is perfection in resurrection,
at the coming of the Lord. Let them do this, and
we will honour them.

With regard to perfection in the sense of being
filled as a vessel, we must remember that capacity
is enlarged by the supply, and the fullest communication of light and power leaves us longing
for more.

Consecration.

THIS is a simple, yet comprehensive term ; solemn in its import, but happy in realization. It is oftener used than understood, and sometimes misapplied. It frequently occurs in the Old Testament, and twice in the New. In both it is applied to persons and things.

It is the translation of different words employed in the original Scriptures, which, taken together, teach—

I. Separation, sometimes absolute and perpetual, to God.

II. Completion, perfection, filling the hands, as in the case of Aaron and his sons.

It is used in the New Testament—

I. In connection with the person of Christ in resurrection. He, the Son, Priest by the word of the oath, is *consecrated*, perfected for evermore (Heb. vii. 28).

II. In relation to His work, as consecrating, *perfecting*, newly-making the way into the holiest (Heb. x. 20).

A few remarks on each of the above may prove helpful to some, especially in connection with true, intelligent worship.

True worship is adoration of God, even the Father, revealed in His Son, the Lamb, by the Holy Ghost—adoration (1) for His personal excellence, (2) for the perfection of His ways, and (3) for His gifts.

As a matter of *experience*, we thank Him for His gifts, admire Him in His ways, and adore Him for His proper personal dignity and glory. This last is the highest point, and implies the lowest estimate of ourselves.

We bow the head, giving thanks for salvation from wrath. With fuller understanding and closer communion, we bow both head and knee. Closer still, and we prostrate ourselves before Him and the Lamb, not in confusion, but confidence; not to beg salvation, nor even to ask forgiveness, but, while conscious of what we were, and of our present imperfection, to adore Him, and make the ascription of sevenfold excellence and glory to the Lamb (Rev. v. 12), giving thanks unto the Father by Him.

Such worship can only be offered by those in and by whom the true idea of *consecration* is realized.

The people of the world cannot, do not, worship. They may assume the name worshipper, learn a true creed, have and frequent a building said to be for worship, and have a man called a priest to lead the forms and perform the ceremonies; but they cannot worship the Father until they are actually separated to God by the new birth, and by faith in the Son of God. Then they cease to be of the world, and are in that Church to which all acceptable worship is confined.

CONSECRATION—GODWARD.

Chosen in Christ before the foundation of the world (Eph. i. 4), sanctified by the blood of Jesus (Heb. xiii. 12), and by the Holy Ghost through faith in Him (1 Peter i. 2), consecration is realized in them and by them in its *first* sense. This *separation to God* is essential, absolute, and abiding.

Circumstances may change, experience vary, service be interrupted, inconsistency in conduct may diminish joy and remove the bloom of communion, but *consecration* in this sense abides. It is God's act, and done for ever.

In such persons, holding their true place before God, the *second* meaning of the term is also exemplified; viz., *perfecting, filling the hand*. Of this the typical ceremony described in Exodus xxix. is the happy illustration.

Redeemed and circumcised persons, as we see from that chapter, were first bathed, effectually cleansed; then on clean flesh were put the priestly garments; after that came the slaying of victims and ordering the offerings; then they were tipped, ear, thumb, and toe, with blood, sprinkled with blood and oil; and, lastly, their hands were filled with an offering to wave before JEHOVAH. Thus they were " consecrated," and they then fed on the offerings.

That which answers to this is now produced by the Holy Ghost.

Sinners redeemed by the blood of the cross, are quickened, regenerated by the Holy Ghost, and enabled to realize their effectual cleansing, the bathing never to be repeated (John xiii. 10). They apprehend by faith Christ as their righteousness before God, and, anointed with the Holy Ghost, present Him to the Father. Their hand is filled with Him in all His fulness and perfection. They speak and sing of Him to the Father, and for Him they give thanks.

Once it was otherwise with them. *Then* they presumed to approach God in nature, in the flesh, having no better covering than their own righteousness, filthy rags; without blood and without oil, and their hand filled with their own religious performances; but they did not worship. Like Cain and the boasting Pharisee in the temple, they were rejected; but now, the Holy Ghost having convinced them of sin, and revealed to them Christ—having emptied their hand and filled it with Him—they are accepted worshippers; yea, such as the Father *seeketh* to worship Him.

This is true of all believers—of the babe as well as of the young man and the father. All are separated to God, and are all consecrated priests to God, even the Father.

That which was true of Levi is promised to the nation of Israel (Exodus xix. 6; Isaiah lxi. 6), and is realized in the election (1. Peter ii. 5-9) in earnest. The priesthood of believers now is universal.

Could we all, beloved, see the beauty and glory of an assembly of such priestly worshippers gathered to the name of Jesus our Lord only, and understand the Father's estimate of their worship, I am sure we should prefer it to all other assemblies, nor should we suffer trifles, anything that could be overcome or set aside, to hinder our being there, especially as surrounding the Lord Himself at His table, to remember His death, in hope of His return.

Believers are Divinely constituted priestly worshippers of the Father. With adoring hearts and joyful lips, they present that offering by which they have been both *sanctified* and *perfected for ever* (Heb. x. 10-14), in which the Divine counsels and operations centred, and the full Deity ever delights; for " CHRIST, through the ETERNAL SPIRIT, offered Himself without spot to God." That offering was a sweet-smelling savour (Eph. v. 2), and will ever be so. He, the great High Priest, is perfected for evermore, and the way into the holiest is newly made, consecrated for us.

CONSECRATION—MANWARD.

Having thus far considered the term " consecration" in connection with worship, and its direct relation to God, I now wish to say a little on it in its practical and manward aspect, properly resulting from and again leading to the former.

In doing this, I shall first refer to a few remarkable passages in the Old Testament in which the expression occurs, and, secondly, consider some of those in the New Testament which convey the idea, or teach this truth.

The earliest in the Old Testament is Exod. xxxii. 29. The sons of Levi, on the occasion of Israel's idolatry and fornication, *separate* themselves, and, at the command of Moses, *consecrate* themselves— fill their hands by slaying every man his son and brother—firm, unflinching, full-handed obedience to Jehovah.

How sad and fearful the connection! But it was simple obedience. They had the warrant of the word of Moses as from Jehovah. We should never act without the guidance of the Word of God; but having it, we should act, whatever may be the consequences to ourselves or others.

Blessed be God, He has not committed the sword to the Church (therefore it should not be found in the hand of any one of its members), although He has transferred it from Israel to the Gentiles. Nevertheless, the claims of the Lord Jesus through His Word may, and often do, call for costly sacrifices and service, painful, yea, as death, to the flesh; nor should we be less true than the Levites were then.

The next passage I shall adduce gives us the

term in a very interesting connection—that of the Nazarite. The Nazarite's vow is very instructive. It was not universal in Israel; nor was it generally commanded. It was not essential to the Israelitish character, nor to his standing in the land. It was a voluntary act of extraordinary, yet happy, devotedness to Jehovah—*separation* from the ordinary tastes and delights of nature.

It was consecration, involving both separation and completion; *i.e., fulfilling* the conditions of the vow of *separation.*

The Nazarite for the time was doubtless a type of Him whose whole life was one uniform exhibition of separation from earth's joys, and of devotedness to God—obedience to His Father's will. It does not in the letter apply to us, but in its spirit and principles should be realized and exhibited by us continually.

We find this word consecration again in 2 Chron. xxix. 33, and xxxi. 6, used in connection with the people's substance, their cattle. Hezekiah, like all godly kings, turned his attention to the temple and its service, to the law and to the priesthood; and, finding that the Levites had suffered want, he commanded the congregation to bring in their offerings, and those offerings were *consecrated* things, separated and devoted to Jehovah, their God.

I will only notice one more passage in the Old Testament in which the term occurs, namely,

Micah iv. 13. This Scripture presents to us Jehovah standing up for Zion, to avenge her wrongs and maintain her rights, when all her enemies shall be subdued, and the spoil, the gain, shall be *consecrated*— devoted to Jehovah. This is in agreement with the original ordinance in Israel, that the spoil of their enemies, when it had been tested and purified by passing through fire or water, according to the nature of it, was to be for Jehovah.

It will be easily seen that the Scriptures quoted here, taken together, teach full surrender to the claims of Jehovah of person and things. Israel was Jehovah's nation ; their possessions were His gifts to them ; and the spoil of their enemies was to be devoted to Him.

In meeting His claims, they found their happiness and wealth ; withholding from Him brought sorrow and want.

There are many, many more Scriptures teaching the same blessed lessons, which my readers can search out for themselves, and will be richly rewarded in the search. My desire in writing this paper, as in all ministry of the Word, is to suggest, and lead believers to search the Word prayerfully in secret. Public ministry was designed to help Christians in private meditation ; not to be its substitute ; and it is a bad sign when it is otherwise.

This said, I pass on to consider the Scriptures of the New Testament for further instruction on this subject. As before stated, the word *consecration* occurs but in two passages, and in them only in relation to the person and work of the Lord Jesus, not in direct connection with our practice.

In the first passage, it is the act of God, with an oath *consecrating* the Son (Heb. vii. 28). In the second, it is Jesus *consecrating* a new and living way into the holiest through the veil of His flesh. These, rightly apprehended, will, of course, affect our hearts Godward, and so indirectly affect our general practice; yet they do not directly apply to, nor does the Holy Ghost use the term *consecration* in the New Testament to enforce that which is now being pressed on us by it.

What, then, is the teaching of the New Testament on this subject?

Its instruction might be summed up in one word, a word with which children's ears are familiar, and which should be to every Christian one of most pleasant sound—*Obedience.*

OBEDIENCE.

Had the Church of God from the beginning better understood its meaning, and steadily, habitually, walked in obedience, we should not now, I think, have heard of "consecration meetings," "higher life meetings," and the like. Such are *high-sounding* words, but they prove the *low* condition of the Church, the general ignorance, worldliness, and weakness of the professed followers of Christ, even as the fifteen or sixteen days occupied in cleansing the temple of old proved the neglect of *daily* cleansing (2 Chron. xxix. 15-20).

But I must proceed to cite a few Scriptures in which this truth is taught, although the term *consecration* is not employed. The first I shall refer to, states the fact on which all the claims of God are based, and all the precepts of the New Testament enforced ; viz., that we are "*redeemed.*"

"Ye are not your own ; for ye are *bought* with a price : therefore glorify God in your body and in your spirit, which are God's" (1 Cor. vi. 19, 20). We belong to Another, and He Who has bought us has simple, absolute possession, and unquestionable right. We are accountable stewards of all we have. If we are bought, we are *separated* to Himself ; if we are His, we should in all things be *devoted* to Him, having a settled purpose to be godly, and to live to God in all things. This is the import of the term consecration.

The next passage I shall notice is very similar to this : "Yield yourselves unto God, as those that are alive from the dead, and your members as instruments (*arms*, for righteousness is armour) of righteousness unto God" (Rom. vi. 13). "Alive from the dead ;" yes, partakers by the Holy Ghost of the life taken up in resurrection by Him who laid it down for the sheep, we are to live our life unto God after the example of Christ ; yielding ourselves to Him as "alive" (this is *separation* from a world of "death"), and our members— eyes, ears, tongue, hands, feet—in the *ordinary* matters of life, as so many instruments of righteousness to God.

Such must of necessity be the life of a *risen* one, *higher* than which cannot be lived here, *lower* than which the Scripture does not put before us; nor should we be satisfied with a lower.

Again, in Romans xii. 1, we are besought, by *mercies* received, to present our body as the servant of the renewed mind, "a living sacrifice;" so that the entire occupation of its members is to be for God, to please and therefore to glorify Him.

In 2 Cor. vii. 1, &c., we are appealed to by the *promises* of God to come out from all that with which Christ has no fellowship, and which does not agree with our character, walk and worship; to "cleanse ourselves from all filthiness of flesh and spirit, perfecting holiness in the fear of God." How simple and plain is all this! Surely if we all were more diligent readers of the Word of God as a whole, reading for *fellowship* with Him and *conformity* to Christ in all things, how natural and unmistakeable it would appear! Paul and his companion were enlarged in heart, and their mouths were opened towards the Corinthian believers, who, being puffed up, were cold and contracted. He called on them for the answer, "Be ye also enlarged," in order to which enlargement they must come out and be *separate* from ungodly, un-Christlike fellowships and practices, *perfecting* holiness.

Such are some of the passages of the New

Testament which present to us our simple obligation (which is our privilege) to do the will of God
who has saved us, of our Father who loves us.   I
will not enlarge, but again ask my readers to search
the Scriptures for themselves; they will easily discover them, and be richly rewarded in *obeying* them.

I would add that I have quoted from the
Epistles, not because the Gospels do not teach the
same thing (see Luke xiv. 26, 27, 33, and elsewhere),
but because the Epistles are largely expositions of
the Gospels, and are, moreover, addresses to the
Church of God, to the Churches of Christ which
were not formed while the Lord Jesus was on
earth (see Matt. xvi. 18).

I would also remind dear fellow-believers of
the blessed fact that we are indwelt by the Holy
Ghost, whose teaching and power are sufficient to
enable us both to discover and do the will of God
in all things.   He will enable us to yield ourselves
unto God as alive from the dead; to present our
body a living sacrifice; to separate ourselves from
all evil, cleansing ourselves from filthiness of flesh
and spirit, and to perfect holiness : in a word, to *obey*,
and so be godly; first in the closet; then in the family
circle and walk ; after that, in service, in the church
or in the Gospel; and, lastly, before the world in all
our transactions with the people of it.

In such a path God will be glorified, Christ
honoured, others benefited, and our own souls made
happy.   Thus may it be with us to His praise !

The Hope of the Church.

I WISH to give you three or four reasons why the hope of the Lord's coming is so pointedly and frequently presented to us in the Word, and so much insisted on by those who hold it.

THE LORD'S OWN PROMISE.

First, because of the distinct promise given by Him Who is coming. When He was about to leave His disciples—the small band who had left their little all for Him, and gathered round His Person—He told them of His coming departure, of His rejection by the world, and of the trials which should befall them. Their hearts were troubled. How did He seek to comfort and cheer them? Not by speaking *first* of the Comforter, the Spirit of wisdom Who should teach them guide them, sustain and give them victory. No; He fixed their hearts upon the end—" I will come again." " I go to prepare a place for you; and if I go and prepare a place for you, I *will come* again, and receive you unto Myself; that where I am, there ye may be also." In the two following chapters, He opens up to them the difficulties of the way, the grace which would be given them, and the persecutions which awaited them. But first of all,

He fixes their hearts on the end—" I will come again."

HIS HEART OF LOVE.

Second, what is the breath of that promise? The very heart of that promise is the outbreathing of His affection for the objects of His love. Observe the last petition in His prayer: " Father, I *will* that they also whom Thou hast given Me, be with Me where I am." Nothing short of the personal appearing of Christ, to receive His Church into His everlasting embrace, can satisfy His heart.

PERFECTION.

Third, we can have nothing in perfection until He come. Whether individually, or collectively as the Church, whether it is the enjoyment of things above, or on the earth itself, perfection stands connected with the coming of the Lord Jesus Christ. We have already known redemption's power put forth on the ground of redemption's price—the blood—in regard to our souls, and we are happy. But what of these poor bodies? We sigh on account of them. When are these ransomed bodies to know their passage from weakness to power, from mortality to immortality, from corruption to incorruption, from shame to honour? It will be when Christ descends from heaven with a shout, and puts His transforming touch upon these bodies, making them like His glorious body. If we know something of conflict, we sigh for perfect conformity to Christ. Will that be when the happy spirit experiences its exodus from this body of conflict? Oh, no. The perfect man is not only the spiritual image of Christ, but also the very image of that body that hung upon the cross in woe, and is now clothed in bright immortality. When He comes, we shall be like Him, spirit, soul and body.

THE UNITY OF THE CHURCH.

Fourth, the unity of the Church, though real, is not now manifested. The unity of the body of Christ exists by Divine power, and never can be touched; but it is not manifested.

When will it be? When the Church's Centre and Head appears in the air? Then it will not only be one, but manifestly one. Then the Church, now so divided, will appear in the image of Christ.

ISRAEL'S BLESSING.

Fifth, we read, and hear, and speak of God's ancient people, the Jews. When are they to have their land and blessing, that which God covenanted with Abraham to give them? When? When He comes, He is to put them in happy possession of their land, make them one people, and be their true Messiah. Then they shall receive Him as their Saviour, and, knowing Him as their King, they shall rejoice greatly.

So whether individual perfection, the manifested unity of the Church, or Israel's blessing be considered, it is *when He comes.* It is not, therefore, without reason that Christ's coming back in Person and glory, is the *hope* of the Church. May we have it burning more brightly in our hearts, and may its blessed effects be seen in our lives! And may we by our speech and actions ever say: "We are waiting, as strangers and pilgrims here, for our Lord's return!"

PATHS OF RIGHTEOUSNESS.

❖❖❖

Salvation's Threefold Cord.

ALMOST all our misapprehensions and mis-
conceptions in truth arise from a one-sided
regard to one particular aspect of it. In
nothing is this more perceptible than in our
thoughts regarding the relation between *the work
of Christ*, which faith immediately realises; and *the
work of the Spirit*, which is gradually developed,
from measure to measure, from grace to grace, from
glory to glory. To illustrate this relation, around
which, as a mighty paradox, hang so many appar-
ently discordant and yet most blessedly harmonised
truths, we would draw attention to the fifth of
Romans; and may the simplicity of God's truth
not be marred by our want of simplicity in the
presentation of it.

The unity of thought in these verses has been
broken by the same Greek word (καυχαομαι) being
rendered by three different words in the places
where it occurs. In verse 2, it is rendered "rejoice,"
in verse 3 "glory," and in verse 11 "joy." In all
these places, and elsewhere generally, we would

use the word *boast,** as conveying a more distinctive meaning.

The chapter begins with the results of faith to the believer in Christ Jesus, viz., *justification* before God, *peace* with God, and *access* to God, all of which are the *immediate* results of faith. By faith also we are brought into the grace of God, and *out* of it we can at all times draw; for out of Christ's fulness have we all received grace upon grace; grace flowing on, as wave upon wave, from the sea of God's infinite love.

The first two verses have to do with our standing in Christ, as the apostle writes, "in which we stand" (ἑστήκαμεν); that is, wherein we have stood, and do always stand; for we are herein pointed back to the Cross, and onward to the glory, our standing being in grace from first to last.

The result of this is, that we have three successive causes of boasting; and we say *successive*, because there is a Divine order in the relative positions they occupy, which we must not lose sight of. We will now take them up in the order in which they are laid before us.

I. The pathway of faith "*through our Lord Jesus Christ,*" whereby a sinner is able at once to make his boast "in hope of the glory of God" (verse 2). There are no steps here, there are no measures;

---

* It is so rendered frequently (see Romans ii. 17, 23; 2 Cor. vii. 14; ix. 2; x. 8, 13, 15, 16, &c.); and it might be thus translated in other passages, such as 1 Corinthians i. 29, 31; 2 Corinthians xii. 1, 5, 6, 9, 11; Galatians vi. 13, 14, where it is rendered "glory," and thereby confounded with other words of very different significance.

all is absolute, and all is perfect. From the horrible pit and the miry clay, he is at once put on the Rock, and sings the new song that has been put into his mouth by his God, as we read in Psalm xl. 1-3, and are taught in Hannah's song when she sings : "He raiseth the poor out of the dust, and lifteth up the beggar from the dung-hill, to set them among princes, and to make them inherit the throne of glory."

There is but one step from the dust to the throne; from the dust into which sin and Satan brought us, to the throne up to which God has taken all who believe in Christ. This is God's first lesson—a complete and perfect salvation, wrought out for all who are "in Christ Jesus," with Whom they have been *quickened, raised up,* and *made to sit* in heavenly places (Ephesians ii. 5, 6). It is that one step that seals for eternity ; a step out of Adam, out of self, out of the flesh, into Christ, the last Adam, the quickening Spirit ; and therefore it places the Christian, by virtue of the Divine union subsisting between him and his glorified Head, in heavenly places in Christ.

Thus, then, can the weakest believer make his boast in Christ, in hope of the glory of God ; a hope that hangs not on himself for its fulfilment and realisation, but on Christ, in Whom it is ful-filled already ; for he who believes is *saved already,**

---

* In Ephesians ii. 5, 8, as elsewhere, it is the *perfect* tense which is used regarding those who believe ; and this tells of a salvation which was accomplished on the Cross, and which is brought down to the present moment—we have been saved, are so still, and ever will be.

even as he who rejects Christ is *condemned already*,
"because he has not believed in the Name of the
only-begotten Son of God" (John iii. 18).

This, then, is faith's starting-point. He who
believes is justified, and therefore forgiven; he is
saved, and therefore has peace; he has access to
God, and is called to stand firm in the grace by
which he has been brought nigh. All this he has
already, irrespective of personal feelings and individual experiences.

II. We have now to trace the pathway of faith
by the Holy Ghost, and His mighty power inworking in all who believe. Living faith works, and
real faith has its experiences. That which has
been given to us in Christ, as an inheritance that
never fails, has to be brought out in the believer
as a personal realisation.

This is the subject of verses 3, 4, and 5, in which
we find steps and stages that rise higher and higher,
showing a progressive development of the Divine
life. This process is the very opposite of that
which we have been contemplating as the first
subject of boasting of those who, like the little
children in John's Epistle, rejoice in the knowledge
of the forgiveness of sin, and therein see clearly
their pathway to the glory secured in Christ.

The verses are as follow:—"And not only so,
but we boast in *tribulations* also: knowing that
tribulation worketh patience; and patience, experience; and experience, hope; and hope maketh

not ashamed; because the love of God is shed abroad in our hearts by the Holy Ghost which is given unto us."

The boasting here is the result of the indwelling of the Spirit of God, in Whom we have been baptised into one body, and Who is now working in us to will and to do of His good pleasure. The steps in the pathway of faith here given are four— tribulation, patience, experience, and hope, thus ending where the former pathway ended ; but how different the course ! It is this difference that we desire to mark, so as to help some who, failing to see it, are apt wrongly to estimate their position, by either setting aside the fact of the finished work of Christ for them, or by forgetting the progressive attainment realised by the inworking of the Holy Ghost.

The result of the former is to shake the believer's hold on the " It is finished " of the Son of God ; and the result of the latter is either practical Antinomianism, or a delusive belief in an immediate attainment, without the steps necessary and appointed for its realisation. This is the king's highway of consecration, the royal road along which all have walked who have become truly set apart for God. This was the path Joseph trod, and in which Job, Moses, David, Daniel, and Paul walked. There is no exception—there can be none ; and this was the pathway of the Son of God Himself, Who learned obedience by the things that He suffered, wherein

He, the Spotless One, has left us sinners an example that we should tread in His steps.

We notice in verse 3, that tribulations are boasted in and gloried over, not because of what they are in themselves, being not joyous but grievous, but because they work out patience, or endurance. The tried one learns to endure; but tribulation implies a process of sorrow and of suffering to which there is attached an "afterward," when the "peaceable fruits of righteousness" are realised by them who are exercised thereby (Hebrews xii. 11). The gold is put into the crucible again and again, before it comes forth meet for the refiner's use. The wine has to be emptied from vessel to vessel, before it becomes fit for the Master's service.

These tribulations meet us in all variety of ways, from the world, from the flesh, and from the devil; but, however they come, faith can glory, and take up the language of Paul, when there was given unto him "a thorn in the flesh," "the messenger of Satan," to buffet him. He felt the needs-be of the thorn; he knew the danger he was in; he was content with the mighty promise given: "My grace is sufficient for thee;" and he was able to say: "Most gladly therefore will I rather glory (or boast) in my infirmities, that the power of Christ may rest upon me."

Thus Paul realised in his own experience what he wrote to the Romans, and tribulation wrought endurance under the all-sufficiency of the promise that attaches to our whole life : " I will never leave thee, nor forsake thee." He who, in 2 Cor. xii., could boast in visions and revelations, had boasted before in chapter xi. of sufferings and perils, of watchings and fastings, that came on him in the path of endurance, as a vessel consecrated to the service of his Lord.

Thus endurance or patience is not fruitless ; it works out *experience*, or proof—a twofold experience, first of God, and then of ourselves.

The trials of the way, when borne in patience, lead to an acquaintance with God, that were otherwise impossible. " Acquaint now thyself with God, and be at peace," expressed a needed counsel to tried Job ; for as ignorance of God is the secret of all our failings, so acquaintance with Him is the secret of all our peace and rest.

But tribulations lead likewise to an acquaintance with our own hearts, not necessarily at all by failings or outward breakings down, but by that acquaintance with self and with the inworkings of a sinful nature that needs ever to be kept down and brought into forcible subjection, at the cost of pain and suffering to him who would so run as to obtain, and so strive as to win the incorruptible crown. These are dark and bitter experiences—the agonies of mortal conflict, that made the life of those worthies of Scripture a battle and a victory. Our experience should be of victory, and not of defeat, albeit a victory attained in a war both costly and bloody, wherein many a cherished thing, near and dear as a right hand, a right eye, or a right foot, has to be cut off and cast away.

If the gate is straight by which we enter, the path is narrow along which we have to walk; as one of old, in giving his experience of the path, says: " In all things commending ourselves as the ministers of God, in much patience, in affliction, in necessities, in distresses, in imprisonments, in tumults, in labours, in watchings, in fastings, in (εν, as before) pureness, in knowledge, in longsuffering, in kindness, in the Holy Ghost, in love unfeigned, in the Word of truth, in the power of God."

These were the conditions and the elements *in* which his path was trod; and he further adds the means by which the path was maintained: " By the armour of righteousness on the right hand and on the left, by honour and dishonour, by evil report and good report "—all equally the means of commending the blessed man of God as His servant. The apostle sums all up with those paradoxes that to faith are so intelligible, and which yet are so difficult to reconcile in the experience of Christians, leading some to deny one side of the paradox, and some to deny the other: " As deceivers, and yet true; as unknown, and yet well known; as dying, and, behold, we live; as chastened, and not killed; as sorrowful, yet always rejoicing; as poor, yet making many rich; as having nothing, and yet possessing all things."

Such were the experiences of him whose life was a real consecration to God; but it was not a short and easy path, and all he could say four years later was: "Not as though I had *already* attained." In Christ he was complete already, but in himself he was not yet complete; for he was *not* "*already* perfected," nor would he be till he had put off the body of death.

But again, are these experiences fruitless? Far otherwise; they work out *hope*. They bring the experienced soul to a hope realised in his own conviction. That which came to him *in Christ*, in all the fulness of a salvation that was "an anchor of the soul, both sure and stedfast, and which entereth into that which is within the veil" (Hebrews vi. 19), now comes as the result of the love of God having been, and still being, day by day, "shed abroad," or poured forth in the heart by means of the Holy Ghost, Who is given unto us.

The reference to the Holy Spirit here deserves special notice, and contrasts remarkably with the words, "by our Lord Jesus Christ," in verse 1. As we have already noticed, this cause of our boasting has to do with the work and the power of the Spirit, leading all who have come to Christ for salvation to the working out of the same salvation in themselves; and thus what was imputed in Christ, is now imparted by the Holy Ghost in the new nature, and in the new life that flows out of it, as in Romans vi. 4.

In the Cross we see the infinite love of God,
forgiving us all our sins, justifying us in Christ,
and making us heirs of His glory; but in the Spirit
sent down by the risen Saviour we have the witness
of a present love, the seal of a present anointing,
whereby the sweet fragrance of Christ is effected
in us, an earnest of that ultimate conformity to the
image of Christ which is the personal destiny and
hope of every child of God.

The Spirit is the earnest of an as yet uncom-
municable glory, the liberty of the glory of the
children of God; and although we have "the first-
fruits" of it, we groan still, for we are saved by
hope; that is (in the aspect under contemplation
by the apostle), our salvation is a matter of hope,
and therefore in the future; for what a man sees and
possesses, he does not hope for (Romans viii. 24, 25).

III. We have lastly to notice the third ground
of the believer's boasting, and that is, GOD HIM-
SELF. This we find in verse 11, where we read:
"And not only so, but we also boast in God by
our Lord Jesus Christ, by Whom we have now
received the reconciliation" (see margin).

This is the highest attainment of the child of
God: he has learned to know God; and this will
be the joy to be known fully hereafter only, when
God will be revealed to our delighted sight, not as
a stranger, but as the God Who called and chose
us in Christ; and Who by His Spirit walked with
us, carrying us, watching over us, and making

Himself known to us every step of our way. What we need is to be found in the condition to get this present revelation. That condition is *obedience.* " If any man love Me," says the Lord, " he will keep My words : and My Father will love him, and We will come unto him and make Our abode with him."

It is to this point that all the pathway through which we are being led is tending, and into which an ungrieved Spirit will ever lead the obedient, waiting soul. The Spirit never leaves ; but the Spirit can only lead our spirits into the conscious fellowship of the Father and of the Son, when we are walking in the light as He is in the light : then have we fellowship one with another ; and John says : " Truly our fellowship is with the Father, and with His Son Jesus Christ." This is our proper fellowship, and let us make its realisation a possibility by walking in the light.

We cannot now further dwell on this glorious theme, but let us seek to abide in this path wherein faith's songs can be sung with holy exultation, and we can say : " My soul doth magnify the Lord, and my spirit hath rejoiced in God my Saviour."

These three sources of boasting and of trium-phant joy to the child of God, form that threefold cord of covenant grace and glory in our triune God—Father, Son, and Holy Ghost—that secure to God and to us the ultimate fulfilment of all that has been promised, sealed to us by Christ in the

blood and in the Spirit.   May we not miss in our
conceptions of truth any one of the strands of this
Divine cord of saving grace, or we shall mar its
beauty and dim the bright light of God's truth
upon our own souls.

The Liberty of Sonship.

BONDAGE and liberty are figures very frequently used in the Word of God. By nature, man, created in the image of God, enjoyed the liberty of a creature in the presence of his God; but when sin came into the world by man's disobedience, he passed under "the bondage of corruption." He was free no longer. Sin was the master; he was the slave. Death was the tyrant; he was the bondsman. Satan was the murderer; he was the victim.

Man of himself never learns this. The Holy Ghost alone reveals it; and when it is revealed, the sinner knows what it is to be lost. Satan's grand deception is to make man think he is free. This flatters his vanity; but behind self, Satan is ever hid. He has usurped God's place, and reigns, perhaps unsuspectedly, in a corrupted will and depraved affections.

In order to break this bondage, the Son of God has come, born of a woman, born under law, to redeem from the bondage of Satan, to save from the power of sin, and to deliver from the fear of death. Christ has come to destroy ($\lambda v \sigma \eta$, unloose or untie) the works of the devil, which, in man, have resulted in a *threefold* bondage; viz., of the *will*, of the *mind* (which includes the intellectual faculties), and of the *affections*. The Lord says, in Jeremiah: "Let not the wise man glory in his wisdom, neither let the mighty man glory in his might, let not the rich man glory in his riches: but let him that glorieth glory in this, that he understandeth and knoweth Me, that I am the Lord which executeth loving-kindness, judgment, and righteousness, in the earth." Jehovah has provided a remedy from this threefold bondage and threefold apostasy. Freedom has been procured by the Son, Who says: "If the Son shall make you free, ye shall be free indeed" (John viii. 36). This is "the liberty wherewith Christ has made us free" (Galatians v. 1), in which we are told to "stand fast," that we "be not entangled again in the yoke of bondage."

The old nature, the flesh, loves its chains still; "it is not subject to the law of God, neither, indeed, can be;" and therefore, as long as we carry about "the body of death," we shall need the redemption-power of the Son of God, through the indwelling of the Holy Ghost, to be continually exercised on our behalf. We too little remember this. We have not sufficiently learnt the lesson of our weakness. We realise not the danger of becoming again entangled with the yoke of bondage. We are prone to act as if the flesh were dead in us, because in Christ we are dead to it; and to imagine that its influence is gone, because its mastery has been set aside in Christ.

Yet, though groaning within ourselves, we are the sons of God, and it will soon be manifested that we are such ; but in the meantime redemption must be laid hold on with a firm grasp, if we would really and practically know what LIBERTY means, and what it involves. Redemption price is the precious blood, and redemption power is the Holy Ghost.

The water from the smitten rock illustrates the latter. The rock could be smitten but once, and that by the rod of the Holy God, Who cried : "Awake, O sword, against My shepherd, and against the Man that is My fellow : smite the shepherd, saith the Lord of Hosts" (Zech. xiii. 7). Henceforth and evermore the command to us all is, as to Moses : " Take the rod [the symbol of Divine power] . . . and speak ye unto the rock before their eyes ; and it shall give forth His water, and thou shalt bring forth to them water out of the rock" (Numbers xx. 8).

It is this that fainting souls need. This it is which gives liberty from the bondage of wilderness circumstances and wilderness trials. This will make the wilderness and solitary place to be glad, and will cause the desert to rejoice and blossom as the rose. We are told : "It shall blossom abundantly, and rejoice even with joy and singing : . . . . . they shall see the glory of the Lord, and the excellency of our God." We may well read and ponder over this glorious chapter of liberty and joy (Isaiah xxxv.), if we would enter into the real liberty wherewith the Lord makes His people free. This is the liberty which the Gospel proclaims to the captive, to whom God would give "*beauty* for ashes, the oil of *joy* for mourning, the garment of *praise* for the spirit of heaviness" (Isaiah lxi. 3). Yes, truly the liberty of Christ *gives* beauty, joy, and praise; and, whether we have stood fast in our liberty or not, it *is* our portion—the very first-fruits of the Gospel to every one that believeth; for "all things are ours," because we are Christ's, and Christ is God's.

The ashes, the mourning, the heaviness, *belonged* to us, as convicted sinners under the teaching of the Spirit of God. They were our proper portion while in the flesh, and again become our practical condition when we fall under the power of the flesh. Then the fallen one needs again the Gospel of liberty to be re-echoed in his hearing, and the presence of the mighty Advocate again to proclaim liberty.

This liberty is not only deliverance from "the *corruption* that is in the world"—from which the Cross once and for ever has separated those who are "partakers of a Divine nature"—but also from "the *pollutions* of the world" in daily life (compare 2 Peter i. 1-4, with ii. 18-22). The liberty of "the Divine nature" is according to a "Divine power," which "has given us all things that pertain to life and godliness;" while the so-called liberty of the old nature is but the bondage of corruption, that returns like "the sow that was washed to her wallowing in the mire." In the one, the human has been made partaker of the Divine, that is, is born again; in the other, the human has been washed, but left unchanged in the bondage of its inward corruption.

But to return. We have observed that in a threefold sense the Son of God is proclaiming liberty from the thraldom of sin over the *will*, the *mind*, and the *affections*. This He accomplishes by making God the Centre of all three, giving to our will His law, to our mind His wisdom, and to our affections His love; and this law, wisdom, and love, find their embodiment in Christ, and their communication in the Holy Ghost. They are objectively presented to us in Christ, and they are subjectively wrought out in us by the Holy Ghost. In God is the essence; in Christ is the manifestation; and in the Holy Ghost is the impartation. The Father gives the Son to reveal Himself, and the Son gives the Holy Spirit (Who proceedeth from the Father and the Son), to communicate Himself; and thereby He brings many sons unto "the liberty of the glory" of the family of God.

Liberty knows of no external coercion. Where that is, there can be no real liberty. All its restraints and constraints are with its full consent.

Of His own will, God loved us, and begat us
through the Word of truth; and when begotten
again, we love Him, because He first loved us.
There is no fear in that love, for there is no
bondage in it. We love, *not* because we ought to
love, *not* because it is consistent with law and
right, but because we cannot help loving. It is
the intuition of the new life. It needs no law, for
it is a law unto itself, just as wives are not *commanded* to love their husbands. Love must flow
down before it can flow back; and the way to
increase our love to our God and Father, is to
remove the hindrances to the inflow of His love
into our hearts, and then it will of necessity rise
again to Himself, Whence it sprang. This is the
liberty of Christ that influences the whole man,
and sanctifies wholly spirit, soul, and body.

Sin brought in fear, and fear truly has torment.
Love drives away fear, and fills the soul of him
who loves, with joy and peace.

Let us now say a few words on this liberty in
the three aspects already named.

First. *The liberty of the will* over the power of
sin. The heart is, we believe, figuratively regarded
in Scripture as the seat of the will. It is that
which in animal life gives energy and power to the
organs of our body. It would be a most instructive
study to trace out in Scripture all that is placed
in connection with the heart, that great depth in
man which God only can search out, which He

only can fathom, and whose streams He only can turn. We are taught to say : " *Thy will* be done;" and when this is said in truth, it proves that God has regained His place in the heart of him who utters it, that He has fathomed the mighty springs of the human will, and brought that will into harmony with His own ; and this *not* by an act of coercive power, but by such a manifestation of Himself that we believe He has no will towards us except for our blessing, and therefore we can have no will but His pleasure.

This is where implicit faith and unhindered trust would place us, and our joyful assurance then would ever be, that all things were working together for good under the all-wise guidance of our God and Father. There would then be no will but God's. This would be our yoke, and we should find it easy, and the burden light.

Thus it would be if the liar, the old serpent, did not beguile us with his whisperings, and his lies, even as he beguiled Eve. It was this that excited Paul's fears for the Corinthian converts, and it is this that may well excite our fears for ourselves, and for one another. Satan beguiles, and, though we are not ignorant of his devices, we often disregard them. " My son, give Me thine heart;" that is, give over to Me thy will, place it under My guidance, subject it to My will. This is God's requirement from us ; and then the full response will ever be, as with the blessed Lord : " Not My

will, but Thine be done." Had it not been so with
Him, what would have been the result? Because
it is so seldom thus with us, what are the consequences? Loss here, and loss in eternity. May
our hearts utter their loving " Amen," as we say:
" Thy will be done on earth, as it is in heaven."

Second. *The liberty of the mind* from the influence
of man's falsely-called science; for the foolishness
of God is wiser than man. " Ye shall be as gods,
knowing good and evil," was Satan's temptation
to Eve; and ever since, the wisdom of the flesh
has exalted itself against the wisdom of God—a
wisdom that makes a man a fool that he may be
wise. We say: " God *only* wise;" if we believed
it more, we should more easily learn the lesson:
" Let not the wise man glory in his wisdom."

We must not confound wisdom with reason.
Wisdom may transcend all our reason; for reason
necessarily has a creature limitation which is too
often lost sight of, and the highest reason is to
bend to a wisdom that often it cannot understand.
It is but reasonable that a child should defer in
things beyond its reach to those wiser than itself,
and it is but reason that in matters beyond our
consciousness we should bow to the wisdom of
God. But here also Satan has come in; and as
he has made man self-willed, so has he made him
proud in his unreasonable claim to a right to judge
of all by a measure of his own.

God is wiser than man; yet God requires not of

us faith in what is contrary to reason, but only in
that which is above our reason. That which now
appears contrary to reason, is only so because of
the limitations that necessarily surround us. Man,
by searching, cannot find out God; and nothing
but the apostasy of the mind from God would lead
the creature to exalt itself against the knowledge
of God—a knowledge given by God, and not to
be found out by the wisdom of the creature.

In contrast with this wisdom which comes up
from beneath, welling up out of the depths of the
darkness of the natural mind, is that which comes
down from above—Christ, the wisdom of God. In
the contemplation of the wisdom of God's ways
in Christ, Paul exclaims: "O the depth of the
riches both of the wisdom and knowledge of God!
how unsearchable are His judgments, and His ways
past finding out! For who hath known the mind
of the Lord? or who hath been His counsellor?
Or who hath first given to Him, and it shall be
recompensed unto him again? For of Him, and
through Him, and to Him, are all things: to
Whom be glory for ever" (Romans xi. 33-36).

None had gone deeper, and none had soared
higher, than Paul, who was taken up into the third
heaven; but he who had sat at the feet of Gamaliel
was now sitting at the feet of Christ, and all his
wisdom became foolishness in the presence of His
Cross. His mind found its liberty, for he could say:
"We have the mind of Christ." The uncertainties

of opinions passed away, and the certainty of
Divine fact occupied their place. Once he could
say, as Naaman of old : " I thought; " but now he
can say also with him : " I know."

Theories in the mind lead to thoughts that rise
like mists and fogs from the swamps and quag-
mires of unbelief; but realisations of life and
health in the soul (the effect of the sevenfold
dipping in the Jordan) lead to a knowledge that
no human wisdom can touch, and no scepticism
assail with success. Infidelity is God's engine
to lay low ungrounded theories. However right
those theories may be, they are unreal to the
doubting soul; however good the material may be,
the house is built on the sand, and it falls.

Third. *The liberty of the affections and desires.*
Sin has come in, and polluted every affection and
every desire. We read : " All that is in the world,
the desire of the flesh, and the desire of the eye,
and the pride of life, is not of the Father, but is
of the world " (1 John ii. 16).

The light of the knowledge of the glory of God
in the face of Jesus Christ, shines into this moral
and spiritual darkness, and the tempest of man's
affections and desires is brought into a great calm
before Him Who walks over its troubled waters,
and says : " Peace, be still." After casting out the
demon from the demoniac, who was so exceeding
fierce that no one dared pass by that way, He
presents the maniac to us sitting at His feet,

clothed, and in his right mind. He was enslaved once, and tyrannised over by Satan; now he is at liberty, and sitting at his Deliverer's feet. He once went as he was driven, as man in the bondage of corruption; he now goes in the impulse of a newly-found freedom, and tells what great things Jesus had done for him, and had had compassion on him.

So was it with us, when in our affections and desires, sin ruled, and "the works of the flesh" manifested themselves; but now Christ rules in the liberty of love, and "the fruit of the Spirit" occupies the place of the works of the flesh. That fruit is "love, joy, peace, long-suffering, gentleness, goodness, faith, meekness, temperance: against such there is no law. And they that are Christ's, have crucified *the flesh, with its affections and desires.*"

Thus, instead of those affections and desires which produce the works of the flesh, those new affections and new desires have come in which mark those who live and who walk in the Spirit; and its precious fruit is brought forth spontaneously through the fruitfulness of living fellowship with the Living Vine. Fruit is not made; it grows, like the lilies of the field, which toil not and spin not; and so the sweetest affections and desires of the soul grow, "fruit of His toil," not of ours.

What fulness of liberty there is here, of well-pleasing fruitfulness to God, that springs spontaneous, as flowers in the wilderness and roses in the desert, through the living waters that flow there!

Thus all is the most perfect liberty; His service is perfect freedom. The *will* is redeemed and brought into liberty, that only finds its freedom in the will of God; the *mind* is redeemed, and finds its liberty in unfolding and in drinking in the infinite wisdom of God; and as the child of wisdom justifies wisdom in all His ways, the *affections and desires* are also redeemed, and find their outflow and their enjoyment in that fruit-bearing unto God, wherein He is glorified, and whence is yielded the wine that rejoices the heart of God and man.

The principle of all heavenly freedom is *obedience;* and hence we read: " I will walk at liberty; for I seek Thy precepts." There can be no liberty elsewhere; all outside it is bondage.

But do we *stand fast* in the enjoyment of the liberty wherewith we have been made free? Are we in any measure entangled with the ill weeds of Hagar's bondage, and of the mind of the flesh, as typified in Ishmael? Have we cast out the bond-woman and her son? It will cost much heart conflict; and unless we rise up early to do it, we shall find them so firmly settled in the house that the probability is we shall never get them out of the house at all, till the house itself be taken down, and "we fly away;" and shall never know how much the spirit of bondage has marred our spiritual life, dishonoured God, and injured our usefulness, until we stand before the judgment-seat of Christ. Then the whole-hearted, who have walked in the liberty of the Gospel, and the half-hearted, who walked in the footsteps of Ishmael that mocked, shall alike know what they have gained and what they have lost.

May God give us all grace to walk in the truth that makes free, and, standing fast therein, see to it that we become not again entangled in the bondage of the flesh.

The Believer's Daily Cleansing.

NO one who has read the blood-stained pages of the Jewish ritual, or who has in faith contemplated the mysteries of the Cross, can for a moment look upon sin as a trifle, a matter lightly to be thought of, or easily to be removed. Its burden has rested as a curse upon man, marring his joys, and pouring poison into his veins, so that the Almighty Sin-bearer cried out, in the agony of the Cross, "My God, My God, why hast Thou forsaken Me?" In the mysteries of redemption, every child of God sees the judgment of sin put away, and in the joy of forgiving love, can say, "There is therefore now no condemnation to them which are in Christ Jesus." But while this is true, a black cloud often arises from a consciousness of indwelling sin, which makes him cry out, "Oh, wretched man that I am!"

In reference to sin, we are exposed to two opposite dangers, which have equally to be guarded against—the one leading to presumption, and the other to despair. It is, however, the former of these that we purpose chiefly to consider, because we think it is particularly needed.

Salvation is free, infinitely free; it is complete

and for ever, so that he who believes can say, "All things are mine, whether life, or death, or things present, or things to come, all are mine; for I am Christ's, and Christ is God's" (1 Corinthians iii. 22, 23). Yet do we read in 1 John i. 9: "If we confess our sins, He is faithful and just to forgive us our sins, and to cleanse us from all unrighteousness." At this "IF" not a few have stumbled; some from introducing uncertainties into the blessed Gospel, where to the sinner "all is yea and amen;" some by making the standing of the child of God in Christ a matter of uncertainty or doubt. These stumbling-blocks are found in the one-sidedness of our perceptions of Divine truth, and can only be removed by enlightenment from above. There is nothing more untrue than truth out of proportion.

It is necessary to observe the force of the "WE" in the verse alluded to. Throughout the Epistles, and particularly the Epistles of John, this word applies to the Church of God as opposed to the world, as in the verse, "WE are of God, and the whole world lieth in the wicked one." Thus the apostle speaks of the children of God, and to them he presents that solemn "IF," as if he would impress on all the deep importance of confession of sin. It seems strange to have to press such a point as this, but it is no less necessary. To confess present sin in order to obtain a present forgiveness, seems, in the minds of some, to be legalism, if not a virtual denial of the atonement; and the result of this tendency is necessarily a low consciousness of present sin, and a dealing lightly often in relation to it, which is alike subversive of personal holiness and of the Divine glory.

Let us, then, remember the solemn truth that unconfessed sin is unforgiven sin. But in saying this, there are two aspects in which forgiveness is to be viewed: the one as affecting the sinner, and the other the saint. In the one case, the unforgiven has no fellowship with the Cross; he is still an alien, a stranger, far off, without hope and without God in the world, and under condemnation. In the other, the unforgiven is a *child*, who cannot enjoy peace as long as sin lies between himself and the Father. This distinction it is most important to bear in mind. A child may be an unforgiven child with respect to particular sin or sins, who may yet have laid his hand on the Cross, and have a right to say, " There is now no condemnation." But when sin darkens the soul of the child of God, and removes the light and joy of salvation far from him, what is God's remedy? Not simply a pointing to the Cross, but a calling for confession. Of this state of unconfessed sin, David says: " When I kept silence, my bones waxed old through my roaring all the day long. For day and night Thy hand was heavy upon me: my moisture was turned into the drought of summer." This was no mistaken experience, no experience founded upon a misapprehension of the power of the atonement; it was like the cry of Paul, "Oh, wretched man that I am!" We have to learn that sin in the child of God is even a more dreadful thing than ever sin in the unconverted can be; for it stands opposed, not to a law of condemnation that must judge the sinner, but to an infinite love that made a rebel a child, and that must save the child, even though through the fire.

The latter chapters of John have been well called the "holiest of holies" of the Gospels; and the well-known scene of the feet-washing, in chapter xiii., is given as if to show us what is ever needed, if we would enter into the secret place of the Most High, into the chambers of the King's infinite love and fellowship. There Christ takes the place of the servant, who, with loins girded, with the towel and the basin filled with water, waits at the door of this most holy place to wash the feet of all who would enter in. Does not this tell us of a daily need for which nothing can compensate—a work to be performed again and again as we come in contact with sin, and our feet thereby become defiled? If this cleansing be not performed for us (and we cannot perform it for ourselves), a barrier is raised up which prevents all access into the presence-chamber of God, and God, in consequence, has again to be viewed as from afar; for not until the soul that came to the *altar*, has come consciously to the *laver*, can there

be a restoration of the joy of lost blessings, and of
the light of an unclouded peace. Let not the
Christian, then, contemplate the possibility of
possessing a sense of forgiveness, unless he is
walking in the light where the blood daily cleanses.
There may be the reality of a judicial pardon, but
the sense of a Father's forgiveness is impossible.

In order to have this truth more deeply written
upon our hearts, let us turn to the ordinance of the
ashes of the red heifer (Numbers xix.) This will
show us unmistakably that while the sin-offering
on the day of atonement pointed to the Cross, on
the ground of which the Aaronic blessing could
come down upon the people of Israel, a particular
ordinance was appointed which provided a daily
remedy, always at hand, to do away with the
uncleanness that man is ever liable to, from within
or from without. There we see delineated the
gracious remedy ordained of God to meet the
necessities of His people's *walk*, as the day of
atonement met the necessities of their *condition*.
The one enables us to walk on our high places, as
the other secured our standing in those heavenly
places in Christ ; telling us that if we are *alive*
in the Spirit, we must also *walk* in the Spirit
(Galatians v. 25).

We will not dwell at any length on the preparation of the ashes of the heifer, or the dust of the
heifer, as it is also called. Like the other sacrifices,
this offering was to be " without spot and without

blemish," typical of Him Who presented Himself
without spot to God. On it must never have come
yoke—the true type of our Lord, Who, from the
cradle to the grave, was the Servant of God, the
obedient Child of the Father. The devil's yoke
never rested on His holy neck; and when Satan
came, the Holy One could say, "he hath nothing
in Me." Once he sought, by the offer of all the
world and all its glory, to lay his yoke upon Him;
but he was met with that reproof, "Get thee behind
Me, Satan." The heifer was also to be red
(*adammah*, in the Hebrew), a beautiful indication
of its connection with mankind; for God formed
man out of the ground (*adammah*, red earth), and,
therefore, called his name Adam. Thus have we a
type of a perfect humanity in Christ; and through
His death (Psalm xxii. 15) came the "*dust*" and
"*ashes*," which, "sprinkling the unclean, sanctifieth
to the purifying," not of the flesh, but of the conscience, as the apostle tells us in Hebrews ix. 13, 14.
It was further ordained that the red heifer, like the
sin-offering, was to be brought forth *without the
camp*, to have its blood sprinkled towards the
sanctuary seven times, to be wholly burnt with
fire, into which was to be cast the cedar, the
hyssop, and the scarlet; and of this offering it is
said, in Num. xix. 9, "It is a sin-offering."* Observe

---

* The English version has "a purification for sin;" the word in the
original is that always used for sin-offering, and it is most important to
retain the word in the chapter before us, as connecting the ordinance with
the sin-offering in Leviticus iv.

further, that every step involved defilement—1st,
of the priest who sprinkled the blood (verse 7);
2nd, of him who burned the heifer (verse 8); 3rd,
of him who gathered the ashes (verse 10); and
lastly, of him who sprinkled the unclean person
(verse 21); while of the sin-offering, on the contrary, it is said, "Whatsoever shall touch the flesh
thereof shall be holy" (Leviticus vi. 27).   There is
a deep mystery in this, the one saying, " He was
made sin," and the other, " He knew no sin," but
" He was made sin *for us*, that we might be made
the righteousness of God *in Him*."

Thus much on the preparation of "the dust"
and "ashes;" but what was to be done with them?
We are told in verse 9, " It shall be for *a-thing-to-
be-kept*" (Hebrew, *mishmereth*).   This word is used
in Exodus xii. 6, of the Passover Lamb, which
was a-thing-to-be-kept from the 10th to the 14th
of the month; and it is also used four times in
Exodus xvi. of the manna, which was something-
to-be-kept throughout Israel's generations in the
golden pot before the Lord, and which was to-be-
kept also on the sixth day, that they might eat it
on the seventh day.   From this we learn that, as
Christ is kept for the Church as the manna of her
daily bread, "the hidden manna," so is Christ
kept for the Church as the ashes of her daily
cleansing.   The daily feeding on the one is no less
essential than the daily employment of the other.
Verse 17 tells us how the ashes were to be used:

" They shall take of the dust of the burnt heifer
of the sin-offering, and they shall put living waters
upon it in a vessel " (see margin). What have we
here but death and resurrection—the dust of death
mingled with the waters of life?—that mystery
which the outpouring of the Spirit of life from the
Lamb slain in the midst of the throne explains.

The yearly atonement, as we have already said,
gave the Israelite access to the sanctuary ; but
that access had to be kept up, and hence the
needs-be for some other ordinance than that of
which the two goats of the sin - offering bear
witness, when one was slain, and the other—the
scape-goat — was sent by a fit person into the
wilderness, bearing away the sins confessed upon
his head. This provision we have in the ashes of
the heifer. It is said in verse 11, that he who
touched the dead body of a man should be unclean
seven days, and so of any one who came into the
chamber of death, or who touched a bone of a
dead man, or his grave. And what does all this
bear witness to, but that all contact with death
defiles ? The dead is but in type the " old man,"
the body of sin and of death, that in the child of
God has been crucified with Christ. To all others
this dead thing is *living*. In every unconverted
man the old man (Adam) is yet alive ; but in the
child of God it has been crucified, and, therefore,
it is said of the saints, " Ye have died;" " The
body is dead because of sin ;" &c. But while this

D

is true, alas! how frequently is the child of God defiled by moral contact with the body, the bone, or the grave, of the old, dead Adam. All such contact defiles; it may happen often unwittingly, yet it is none the less defiling, and it is just this that the ordinance under consideration is calculated to meet.

As we have seen, the ashes were kept for Israel, and a clean person had to take of them, and to mix then and there with living water, and then to sprinkle the unclean. Observe, it was not to be mingled until the time of need came; the water of separation could not be reserved for future use, as were the ashes of the heifer, thereby conveying precisely the same truth as the ordinance as a whole teaches—that present uncleanness needs a present remedy; as it is so beautifully said in 1 John i. 7, that "the blood of Jesus Christ His Son cleanses [or is cleansing] from all sin." This action of the blood on the conscience is very precious. It is not a past "*hath cleansed,*" but a present "*is cleansing,*" that we need to be made conscious of.

We now come to the solemn warning voice, "He that purifieth not himself, defileth the tabernacle of the Lord; and *that soul shall be cut off* from Israel: because the water of separation was not sprinkled upon him, he shall be unclean: his uncleanness is yet upon him."

It may be asked, "Does not this militate against

the security of the position of the child of God?" Our reply might be, " We have merely to present the whole truth of God, withholding nothing, though our ignorance sees not how it can be made consistent with another aspect of Divine truth." We will, however, observe, for the sake of the weak, that God knows how to deliver His children out of Sodom, and He can bring them through untold sorrows to that point when their defilement becomes confessed, where they must confess or die, and where application is made to the Clean One, the Holy and the True, to sprinkle " clean water " that they may again be clean, and that they may enter at last the haven of rest; even though it be as in a barque dismasted, and well-nigh a wreck, that the mariner—" scarcely saved " —enters into port.

Let us seek, by walking in the light, as He is in the light, and by having constant recourse to God's ever-sufficient remedy for all defilement, to secure to ourselves an abundant entrance into the everlasting kingdom of our Lord and Saviour Jesus Christ.

While the soul is saved " yet so as by fire," who can describe the present terribleness of that sentence, " cut off from Israel," which has been quoted, and that expression which is its counter-part, "*no part with Me,*" of John xiii ? Can we be surprised that when immediate, daily application in faith is not made to Jesus, the Friend Who

is clean, and ready to sprinkle the unclean, a
sense of distance and of separation is felt between
the soul and God? Is it to be wondered at? A
present application of the ashes and the water is
needed; yea, we need as consciously to have our
hearts sprinkled with "clean water," as we did in
the first instance, as sinners fresh from the world,
to be brought consciously to the holy altar.

The clearer our views of the altar and its ser-
vices may be, the greater is the need of carefulness,
lest "the laver and its foot" be lost sight of. Here,
as everywhere, we have much need for watchfulness, lest one truth displace another, and, therefore, the great importance of typical Scripture,
where God, speaking unto us as unto children,
draws pictures of vital truths which otherwise we
are apt to lose sight of, in their relation to one
another.

The daily walk, the daily cleansing of the conscience, is no less a solemn concern to the child of
God than was his first coming to God through
the blood of the everlasting covenant; and hence
the force of that word in Peter, "to Whom *coming*"
(1 Peter ii. 4). Many who would shrink from
putting sorrow for sin in the place of the atonement in the first instance, seem not to perceive
that there is an equal reason to guard against
putting it in the place of the daily cleansing, as if
any water could cleanse, whether Abana or
Pharpar, other than the living water and the ashes

of the heifer which God has appointed. Alas! how many saints go mourning all the day, walking in darkness, self-inflicted, and bordering on despair, because they realise not Jesus as their sanctification as they have already realised Him as their justification. It is worthy of notice that the apostle connects the act of sprinkling the ashes of the heifer with sanctification rather than with justification (Hebrews ix. 13).

In conclusion, we would again remark that sin in the child of God cuts off from communion, and that the only remedy is Christ, Who will daily sanctify, and thereby render possible that which is so essential to our happiness, as well as to our holiness, even to live and walk nearer and nearer to God. There are, alas! many who are content to live afar off, and such we would only remind of that solemn Scripture which ends with, " And they are *nigh* unto cursing, whose end is to be burned." But to all who have known the constraining power of love we would say : Be not content with anything short of the very innermost circle of that holy communion which has many circles and untold measures ; in time and in eternity, seek to be among the chosen " three," remembering that of some it was said, " They attained not unto the *first three*."

The Anointing.

THERE are subjects in the Word so solemn and so profound that one dreads almost to write of them, lest by profane touch one should desecrate the precious truth that one desires to hallow. Among these stand pre-eminent those truths which are connected with the Holy Spirit, either in His personality or in His operations. Among these mysterious operations, we may mention the quickening, the indwelling, the sealing, the baptising, and the anointing, in all of which God is the Author, through the Lord Jesus Christ, by the communicating grace of the Holy Spirit. That which God the Father purposed, and God the Son wrought out by His incarnation, death, resurrection, and glorification, is made effectual in the believer by the power of the Holy Ghost.

The subject we purpose to touch on here is the *anointing;* and while we seek the pen of a ready writer, we pray for a heart penetrated with the solemn truth that we have been made partakers of quickening grace, and therein possessors of a Divine nature, which renders possible what were otherwise impossible, and which brings the believer into a position that would else be blasphemy to contemplate.

The apostle John tells us that we "have an

anointing from the Holy One " (1 John ii. 20); and again (verse 27): " The anointing which ye have received of Him abideth in you, and ye need not that any man teach you : but as the same anointing teacheth you of all things, and is truth, and is no lie, and even as it hath taught you, ye shall abide in Him " (*i.e.*, Christ ; see next verse). Thus the great point in the Spirit's teaching here, is to *abide* in Christ. He taught us so to abide as His first lesson, and He teaches the same as the daily lesson of the believing soul.

This anointing is one of the grand distinguishing marks of the wonderful dispensation under which we live—a dispensation far more wonderful than than that of sign and miracle which have passed away. In order to form an adequate conception of what this anointing involves, we need to contemplate it as revealed to us in relation to Christ as the Head of the Body—the Church ; and, as we ponder, let us remember the Saviour's words : " As Thou hast sent Me into the world, so have I also sent them into the world." Thus shall we be prepared to understand that mighty promise : " Verily, verily, I say unto you, he that believeth on Me, the works that I do shall he do also ; and greater works than these shall he do ; because I go unto My Father. And whatsoever ye shall ask in My Name, that will I do, that the Father may be glorified in the Son."

His name was THE CHRIST, the Anointed

One of God; and as such we read of Him: "God anointed Jesus of Nazareth with the Holy Ghost and with power: Who went about doing good, and healing all that were oppressed of the devil; for God was with Him" (Acts x. 38). He was God's CHRIST, and His people were Divinely "called *Christians*," as the name whereby God wished His anointed family to be known (Acts xi. 26), to which Peter also alludes in his epistle; for the anointing is not only for service and for power, but likewise for suffering.

This anointing, as we find it described in the prophecy of Isaiah, has reference to character and to service. The passages to which we refer are in Isaiah lxi. and xi.: "The Spirit of the Lord Jehovah is upon me; because Jehovah hath anointed me to preach good tidings unto the meek; He hath sent me to bind up the broken-hearted, to proclaim liberty to the captives, and the opening of the prison to them that are bound; to proclaim the acceptable year of the Lord, and the day of vengeance [retribution] of our God; to comfort all that mourn; to appoint unto them that mourn in Zion, to give unto them beauty for ashes, the oil of joy for mourning, the garment of praise for the spirit of heaviness" (Isaiah lxi. 1-3).

"The Spirit of Jehovah shall rest upon Him, the Spirit of wisdom and understanding, the Spirit of counsel and might, the Spirit of knowledge and of the fear of Jehovah; and shall make Him of quick understanding [margin: scent, smell, *i.e.*, intuition] in the fear of Jehovah: and He shall not judge after the sight of His eyes, neither reprove after the hearing of His ears," &c. (Isaiah xi. 2-5).

The latter quotation shows the Divinely-developed character of the Man Christ Jesus, Who, under the mighty anointing of which He was partaker, grew in stature, and in knowledge, and in favour. What comes to us in regeneration was *His* as the Holy-born from His mother's womb; and as such we would contemplate what the anointing implies, what are its manifestations, and what its fruit, in those of whom it can be said that they have been anointed of God, as Paul tells the Corinthians they were (2 Corinthians i. 21).

In Revelation v. 6, the Lamb of God is described as "having seven horns and seven eyes," and these are "the seven Spirits of God sent forth into all the earth." This description is the more remarkable, as Isaiah xi. has special reference to the coming kingdom and to the glory of the advent, to which the vision in Revelation v. is preparatory. This connection, however, deserves special notice, as it has to do with the mission of the Spirit of God, Who thereby prepares His agents for the work that has to be accomplished by them. We would also connect these passages with "the seven lamps of fire burning before the throne" (Rev. iv. 5), and this again with the seven-lamped candlestick in the holy place.

The Spirit of the Living God is the anti-type of the oil for the anointing, and of the oil for the light. The connection between light on the one hand, and life, love, and power on the other, seems to embrace both sides of the truth of God; as the three branches on the one hand, and the three branches on the other, connected with the centre shaft, unite to form the seven rays of the one Light that burns before God, sending its rainbow glory around the throne, as the harbinger of an eternal covenant fulfilled in Christ.

Let us, then, consider the seven Divine characteristics of the Spirit's anointing in the order in which they stand in Isaiah xi., which we will present in the following manner :—

(1) The Spirit of Jehovah;

(2) of Wisdom   and (3) Understanding;
(4) of Counsel   and (5) Might;
(6) of Knowledge and (7) Fear of the Lord.

These characteristics describe what the Spirit of God is, and what He gives to those anointed by Him, thereby to prepare them for their life, walk, and ministry, even as the Lord Jesus, through the eternal Spirit, accomplished the work given Him to do.

The first feature of this anointing is its Divinity. It is the Spirit of the Living God Himself. On this all hangs—all the efficacy and all the suitableness for the infinite need that has to be met, and the infinite work that has to be done. The work,

whether accomplished *in* us or wrought *by* us, has
to be done by the mighty Spirit of God, Who
worketh all after the counsel of His will. But it
must not be forgotten that it is the Spirit of the
covenant-keeping Jehovah; for that precious Name
has always a connection with God as the "I AM,"
of all that He has purposed and promised. Hence
Genesis ii., which views creation in the light of an
eternal purpose, contains the oft-repeated designa-
tion, "Jehovah God;" while chapter i., which
regards creation as the act of Divine power only,
has the single expression, "God," or Elohim.
"Elohim" reveals God as the God of might and
power; "Jehovah" reveals Him as the God of
covenant and purpose. "Elohim," we read,
"created man in His own image, in the image of
Elohim created He him; male and female created
He them." But when God's ultimate purposes
and designs are contemplated, and to be unfolded,
or rather enfolded in mystery to us, we read in
chapter iii.: "Jehovah Elohim formed man of the
dust of the ground, and breathed into his nostrils
the breath of life;" and further, after the rib had
been taken from man, it is said: "And of the rib
which Jehovah Elohim had taken from man,
builded He a woman" (see margin, verse 22).*
Thus do we connect together the covenant-purpos-
ing Jehovah of Genesis ii. (Who creates Adam and

---

* Nineteen times in chapters ii. and iii. do we get "Lord God," and
never once "God" only, except in the lips of the serpent.

Eve each in a different way, and each in view of a revelation of Himself in Christ, to be made in the fulness of time), with the Spirit of anointing glory that rested on Christ, from Whom it flows down to all His members. Thus the holy anointing oil on Aaron's head flowed down to Aaron's beard, touching the jewelled breast-plate with Israel's names engraven on it, and going down to the very skirt of his garment (Psalm cxxxiii).

Bearing in mind that the essential feature of the anointing is that it is "the Spirit of Jehovah" that anoints, let us now come to the three pairs of branches. The first of these is said to be "the Spirit of *wisdom* and *understanding*." The connection between the two characteristics in each pair deserves particular attention; and it will be found that while one has an *inward* feature of height and depth, the other has an *outward* feature of length and breadth; and the mutual harmony and correspondence bear double witness that the anointing is *of God*. There is much that names the Name of Christ, the Anointed One, that has not this double testimony. But God's foundation, and all that is Divinely built upon it, "standeth sure, having this seal: The Lord knoweth them that are His. AND, Let every one that nameth the Name of Christ, depart from iniquity."* This is God's foundation, on which the Church of the

---

* This seal contains two truths, both of which are needed to prove the impression genuine. One refers to "*The Lord*," and the other to "*Him that nameth*"—a double signature to the covenant bond.

Living God rests in the midst of the apostasy contemplated in this second epistle to Timothy. This
is the seal, and this is the anointing wherewith
God seals and anoints, and whereby He "estab-
lisheth us unto (εις) Christ" (2 Corinthians i. 21).

Wisdom is that inward spiritual faculty which
James tells us comes from above (chapter iii. 17);
and Proverbs viii. is the great key-passage to this
subject, unfolding to us what wisdom is. But here
and elsewhere understanding is connected with it.
Understanding has to do with the outward exhibition of wisdom, or the putting it into exercise and
use. Thus wisdom, when of God, can say: " I
am understanding" (Proverbs viii. 14). Without
wisdom there can be no understanding ; but without
understanding wisdom would be useless. Like
faith and works, they must not be alone ; for that
which is alone is dead.

Wisdom and understanding combined, form the
first development of the anointing, after its Divine
character has been unfolded. He who possesses
it has an infallible guide that at once testifies to
what is of God, and to what is not of God; for
love is keen to understand, and is wise to know.
Hence, he who has the anointing, needs not that
any should teach him as to what is of God, and
what is not of God. He carries the verdict within
himself. He may be ignorant, and may need
teachers to teach him; uninstructed, and need
others to unfold hidden mysteries ; but the power

of detection of truth and error, of light and darkness, rests with those who are anointed with the Spirit of wisdom and understanding. Hence, the most uninstructed saints may be the most Divinely taught. They taste, they see, and receive, according as what they see agrees with the Divine revelation. Hence, wisdom is justified of *all* her children, if only the eye be single, and the heart and will subject to God. If otherwise, the glory of the anointing is lost ; folly takes the place of wisdom, and misunderstanding leads astray.

1 John ii. 18-28 is of special value here. It shows how the " little children " (*i.e.*, babes, παιδια) are raised above all the deceivers that may come in, and all those who may seek to subvert the truth of God ; they have a prerogative of wisdom and understanding to detect all falsehood, and unmask all deceit. They have it, because God and His anointing are with them ; but on them lies the responsibility of *abiding in Christ.* All rests there ; and only as we abide in Christ will the wisdom we have in Him (1 Corinthians i. 30) become an understanding wrought in us by the Holy Ghost, making us truly wise and understanding in the ways of God.

We now come to the second pair of characteristics of this blessed anointing, whereby we are prepared for our priesthood to God, and for our service here—" *The Spirit of counsel and might.*"

It is important to note the combination here, and to observe how it corresponds with the character

of God, of Whom it is said that He is "wonderful in counsel, and excellent in working." What
would counsel be without the might to carry it
into action ? And what would the might be without
the counsel to direct it ? It is the union of these
that consummates the excellence of the Divine
counsels and workings ; and it is the want of it
that so often frustrates our plans and purposes.
Hence, the importance of this Divine combination
in the anointing of the Spirit of God, whereby
the servant of God becomes neither barren nor
unfruitful.

What a consolation, amidst the perplexities of
life, to have in the anointing a counsel of Divine
wisdom that need never fail, and would never fail
if faith but laid hold on that which is freely given
to us of God ! For as Christ is given by the
Father, so is the Spirit given by Christ. Christ
is the gift of God, the Source out of which the
living water, the Spirit of the Living God, flows
unto us. *He* is the Fulness out of which we have
all received, and may be always receiving.

He Who is "the Counsellor" is also "the
Mighty God," the Son that is "*given*" unto us
(Isaiah ix. 6). Oh, could we only thus realise the
gift of God, and make use of the gift by faith, we
should never be in uncertainty when called to act,
and never be powerless in execution ! He is the
" Wonderful," upon Whose shoulders rests the
government of all our little concerns, as well as of

all the greater ones of the Church and of the world. What is ours in Christ, is ours personally and subjectively by the anointing and inworking of the Holy Ghost.

The full realisation of this would enable the trusting soul at once to be content to wait as long as any uncertainty lasted, knowing that when the time for action arrived, the needed counsel would necessarily be forthcoming, if only there were the readiness to obey. He who desires to do shall know (John vii. 17), is a promise of unlimited application ; and he who believingly lays hold on it, can afford to wait, knowing that "in the end," at the right time, "it shall speak and not lie;" and therefore God's Word ever is: "Though it tarry, wait for it ; because it will surely come, it will not tarry " (Habakkuk ii. 3). What rest this assurance conveys to the heart ! what peace ! when otherwise all is restless confusion.

God will not leave an obedient, willing child of His in the dark, *when* the time for action comes. Till then, patient, peaceful waiting on God is required of us, in the calm conviction that in due time God will point out the way. What lessons of dependent grace would thus be learnt ! We may often have to remain, as our Master had, two days in the same place (John xi. 6), even though life and death may seem to hang on our delay ; but we should then never be too late, and never too early.

As, however, the anointing secures to us counsel, so does it secure might. The anointed one learns by faith to say with Paul: "I can do all things in Christ Who strengtheneth me." We should hear nothing of the impossibilities of the Christian life in anything to which we are called of God, for all would be found to be possible to him that believeth. Faith says with the Psalmist (for in the Psalms Christ tells us His experiences for the comfort of our souls): "By thee I have run through a troop; and by my God have I leaped over a wall" (Psalm xviii. 29).

Hebrews xi. gives us a witness to the power of faith in the lives and deaths of those mighty men of God who had both counsel and might for the life of faith and all its issues, whether of conquest or of suffering, of life or of death; whether, like Abel, to bleed by the side of his altar; or, like Enoch, to be translated without seeing death.

Faith places itself at the absolute disposal of another, and triumphs in His will, whether to escape the violence of fire, or to fall under the sharpness of the sword. Faith finds counsel and might under all circumstances, as a part of its anointing and consecration, triumphing alike in deliverance or in death. God's anointed ones stand before Him, and if they live, they live unto Him; and if they die, they die unto Him. And let us remember the apostle's word: "Quit you like men, be strong."

E

The last pair of characteristics is, "*The Spirit of knowledge and of the fear of the Lord.*" Here again it is of the utmost consequence to notice the combination, and also the order in which knowledge and fear stand. The tree of knowledge has taught us what knowledge without fear can do; and all around us we see daily proofs of what unsanctified truth can accomplish, puffing up the mind of the creature, which, like the cold light of night's moon, speaks of death rather than life. In sunlight we have light and heat; and all knowledge that comes from God combines both to the believing soul. We look around in the Church of God, and see the withering effect of light that lacks warmth, of knowledge that lacks fear.

The essential element of our life is godly fear— a fear that trembles at God's Word, a love that fears, lest it disobey. When God singles out the man with whom He will dwell, it is not the man who has the deepest insight into His truth, not the man who understands all knowledge and all mysteries, not the man of the highest intellect, but the man who is of an humble and contrite spirit, and who trembles at His Word. When pride gives place to trembling, and self-assertion to meekness and lowliness, when love trembles and godly fear seeks to obey, then, and then only, are knowledge and the fear of the Lord linked together, as they were in their full perfection in the Person and in the anointing of the Holy One of God.

These combined, form part of the holy anointing oil wherewith we are anointed ; and in the measure in which we manifest these gracious gifts and operations of the Spirit of God, in that measure is the anointing abiding in us. Man can counterfeit many parts of the anointing ; many of its separate features can be imitated by man in the flesh ; but the combination here given never can be found but in the really anointed of God (see Ex. xxx. 22-33).

What terrible shipwreck has been made of some of the most precious truths of God's Word, by knowledge and fear being displaced in their relation the one to the other ! When held together, they will always humble and lay in the dust the one in whom they co-exist. If this were remembered, it would bring down many high pretensions, and many high claims of superiority would crumble into dust. He who is the humblest is the highest, for One has said it Who cannot lie ; and he who has most of the Divine knowledge will be the lowliest and the meekest. The devil *knows ;* but with him knowledge is combined with subtlety, and not with fear ; and this distinguishes knowledge from above and from beneath. He cares not how much we know : if only the heart be filled with pride, he has gained his object ; for he has marred the beauty of the Divine reality. God's truth has lost its life ; God's life has lost its love.

Every step in the life of Christ shows the blending of all these varied features of the anointing,

and we need to seek special grace that we fail not
in the entirety of this most perfect description of
the anointing of Christ, which, like the precious
oil on the head of Aaron, that came down to the
very skirts of his garment, flows down from our
Head to the least and lowest of His members.

Such, then, are the characteristics of our anointing ; and now for a few words as to the result of the
anointing in the anointed ones. It will make them
"of quick understanding" (*i.e.*, of good scent) "in
the fear of the Lord," and the bright intuition of a
living knowledge will raise above the sight of the
eyes, or the hearing of the ears. There will then be
power in service to preach the Gospel to the meek,
to bind up the broken-hearted, to proclaim liberty
to the captive, and the opening of the prison to
them that are bound, to proclaim the acceptable
year of the Lord, and the day of vengeance of
our God.

Such is the life and ministry for which this holy
anointing prepares; it is not given to all to be
manifested in the same way, but it is given to all for
one end—to meet the miseries, sorrows, and darkness of a ruined earth, and to minister to every
needy soul God's only remedy—CHRIST, as presented in the power of the Holy Ghost.

Those thus anointed are priests of the inner
sanctuary, and are enabled by reason of it worthily
to fulfil their place as priests. Thus we read:
" And Moses took the anointing oil, and anointed

the tabernacle and all that was therein, and sanctified them. And he sprinkled thereof upon the altar seven times, and anointed the altar and all his vessels, both the laver and his foot, to sanctify them. And he poured of the anointing oil upon Aaron's head, and anointed him, to sanctify him " (Leviticus viii. 10-12). And further on (verse 30), we read : " And Moses took of the anointing oil, and of the blood which was upon the altar, and sprinkled it upon Aaron, and upon his garments, and upon his sons, and upon his sons' garments with him ; and sanctified Aaron, and his garments, and his sons, and his sons' garments with him."

Leviticus viii. shows the effect of the anointing as preparing for priestly service to God ; Isaiah lxi. shows the power of the anointing in the service to be rendered in the world.

Prophets, priests, and kings, were all anointed with holy oil ; so was Christ for this threefold ministry ; and so are His people now anointed for the same ; and hence our responsibility to maintain anointing power as priests, prophets, and kings ; for thereunto have we been called.

Satan "The Prince of this World."

BEFORE threading our way through the dark subject of Satanic power and rule, it will be well to draw courage for our investigation of this terrible reality by seeing what Scripture says of God's relation to this world, which He made to show forth His praise.

Let us begin with this. All authority and power is from God. He it was Who divided to the nations their inheritance, and set the bounds of the peoples, placing some north, some south, some east, and some west, with relation to Israel's land, which was to be in the midst (see Genesis x. 5, and Deuteronomy xxxii. 8). It was God Who gave Mount Seir to Edom, the land of Egypt to the son of Ham, and the countries of the western seas to the sons of Japheth. Hence, when Daniel stood before the king of Babylon, and told him his dream, he drew from him the confession, " Your God is a God of gods, and a Lord of kings ; " and afterwards, when Nebuchadnezzar had reaped the fruit of his pride in a seven years' deposition from his kingly throne, he learned that " the Most High ruleth in the kingdom of men, and giveth it to whomsoever He will;" for His "dominion is an everlasting dominion, and His kingdom is from generation to generation" (Daniel iv. 32, 34). And Daniel told godless Belshazzar, as he interpreted for him the handwriting on the wall, that it was the Most High God Who gave Nebuchadnezzar "a kingdom and majesty, and glory and honour."

Thus the nations of the earth hold their power at the will of God. Paul tells us in Romans xiii. that their rulers are His ministers; "for there is no power—εξουσια * (*exousia*)—[authority] but by God, and the powers [authorities] that be are ordained of God." The actual holder of the authority may be a Pilate or a Nero, and yet of each we may say, "Thou couldest have no authority . . . except it were given thee from above" (John xix. 11). They hold their authority from God, and we are bound to submit to it in all that contravenes not His supreme will. At the same time, each act they perform, each command they give, emanates from themselves, and is the outcome of that which is of the earth. Hence, unregenerate man rules his fellow-man by the appointment of God, Who yet overrules all, to the accomplishment of His purposes. It is thus that God is the ultimate Governor of nations, though man "meaneth not so" (Isaiah x. 7).

---

* It is well to render this word always "*authority*," to distinguish it from "power" as an act of might. Authority points to what is according to law and under its restrictions.

It may be asked, If man's will acts, how can God rule? With the *how* we have nothing to do. It is impossible for us to say *how* wicked hands of sinful men, carrying out to the very fullest their own will, were, nevertheless, fulfilling God's predetermined counsel at Calvary, but so it was (Acts ii. 23). Pilate was acting on his own authority, the chief priests were carrying out their own designs of envy and murder, and Judas was acting his own part of covetousness and treachery; but while the sin and wickedness rested solely with man, we see in the Cross of Christ God's act as well as man's; for He Who had taken upon Himself our sins, and was unrighteously smitten of man, was righteously smitten of God, because He became the sinner's Substitute. The smiting was the same, the object essentially different.

Extend this principle through the whole course of human affairs, and it will be found to satisfy the Christian who is willing to guide his thoughts by the Written Word, although the infidel may seek thereby to make God the author of sin.

Hence, is it not true that *all* authority, and *every form* of government, good or bad, is subject to God? The unrighteous rulers of nations, the most highly civilised (or " Christianised," as some would say), are " God's ministers," and so are the lawless rulers of savage tribes; for God has no more resigned His government in one corner of the world than He has in another. He rules through His appointed ministers as much in Central Africa as in Europe, whether they be the occupants of a Roman throne, or the wielders of a savage despotism. Authority, power, and rule, are either of God everywhere or of God nowhere. From the fall, when God subjected the woman to the man, and Abel the younger to his elder brother Cain, authority has been from God, whether in the hand of the murderer Cain, or in that of David, the man after God's own heart.

God even says, "Shall there be evil in a city, and the Lord hath not done it?" (Amos iii. 6); and, "I form the light, and create darkness: I make peace, and create evil: I, Jehovah, do all these things" (Isaiah xlv. 7). The moral evil rests with the creature, the physical evil with God, either directly, as the result of His immediate action, or indirectly, as the result of those laws which God has implanted in nature.

Let us now consider what Scripture says of Satan, and of his relation to the government of the world. God has not left us in darkness on this important matter. Our Lord gives us the key to it when He three times calls him "the prince of this world" (John xii. 31; xiv. 30; xvi. 11). The word here translated "prince" is *archōn*, also frequently rendered "ruler," "chief;" it is likewise employed by the Apostle Paul when he says, "Which none of the *princes* of this world knew" (1 Corinthians ii. 8), referring to this world's kings

and rulers. Our Saviour's use of this word prevents our regarding it as an empty title or an
assumed authority not possessed in reality.

He who is "prince of this world" is also called
"the prince of devils" or demons (Matthew ix.
34; xii. 24, &c.), and "the prince of the power of
the air, the spirit that now worketh in the children
of disobedience" (Ephesians ii. 2). In connection with this word (*archōn*) we have the corresponding word principalities (*archai*), used alike of
God's dominion (see Ephesians i. 21 ; iii. 10 ;
Colossians i. 16 ; ii. 10), and of Satan's (Ephesians
vi. 12 ; Colossians ii. 15). Paul tells us that "we
wrestle not against flesh and blood" (that is,
human enemies or human rulers), "but against
principalities [*archai*], against powers [authorities
—*exousiai*], against the rulers of the darkness of
this world [world-rulers of this darkness], against
spiritual [hosts of] wickedness in high [heavenly]
places." Thus we see that Satan's relation to
the world, and to man, as well as to evil spirits, is
one of authority, of power, and of rule.

We cannot now enter into what Scripture says
of *the way* in which he became possessed of it, but
content ourselves with the *simple fact* that the
devil has an authority and a princedom acknowledged by the Son of God, Who, as One "mighty
to save," came to deliver his *lawful* captives (see
Isaiah xlix. 24) from his grasp. Pharaoh as a type
very clearly explains this. Israel went down into

Egypt, into Pharaoh's land, sent there by God for discipline; and when the time of the promise drew nigh, we read that Pharaoh sought to destroy the male children; but doubtless the devil had a deeper purpose, and sought in this way to destroy the promised Seed. Pharaoh here becomes the type of Satan, the prince of this world. As a ruler, he exercised a lawful right over those who dwelt, and had multiplied, in his land. But God holds His claim as paramount, and sends the message, " Let My people go." Still, He does not ignore the fact that Egypt was Pharaoh's land; and it was not until He had in type redeemed Israel by blood, that God put forth His mightier power and brought them out of it. Thus Israel could sing, " Thou in Thy mercy hast led forth the people which Thou hast *redeemed.*" Pharaoh and all his host dead on the sea-shore presents to the eye of faith all Satanic claims against us answered, and all his authority over us set aside for ever. In Exodus xiv. we see in type the fulfilment of what we read in Colossians ii. 15: " Having spoiled principalities and powers" (or better, *having divested Himself* of them as a man divests himself of a garment), " He made a shew of them openly, triumphing over them in it" (the Cross). Thus God triumphed over Pharaoh in the Red Sea ; and God's ultimate triumph for us is eternally *secured* in the Cross, and will be manifested in fact and by power in the fulness of time. For this

Jesus is waiting, as He sits at God's right hand, till His enemies be made His footstool.

While, however, Satan's authority and power are now, by the Cross, set aside for all who have come to Christ, it is otherwise with those who are still Egyptians in nature, and of the seed of the flesh. Of all who believe in Him, we are told that the Father, Who made them "meet to be partakers of the inheritance of the saints in light," hath already delivered them "from the power [authority] of darkness" (*i.e.*, of Egypt, the world, and Satan), and translated them "into the kingdom of the Son of His love: in Whom we have redemption through His blood, the forgiveness of sins" (Colossians i. 12-14).

Of this Satanic "authority of darkness," it is hard for us to write. Our blessed Master felt the terrible coils of its serpentine power when He said to those who came to take Him in Gethsemane, "This is your hour, and the power [authority] of darkness." This power is acknowledged in the first communication made to Satan in Genesis— "Thou shalt bruise His heel." It is a power and a right exercised by the prince of darkness on the heel of the Seed all through the ages; for, though the first advent has secured the redemption, it is only the second advent that can secure the establishment of God's final dominion. Till then the prayer is, "Thy kingdom come; Thy will be done;" for all creation groans under the tyranny of Satan, as John writes: "The whole world lieth in wickedness," or "the wicked one," as in the embrace of a serpent. "The strong man armed keepeth his palace," and "his goods are in peace." The world is the palace of the great enemy. Individuals innumerable are being taken out of his dominion, and translated into the heavenly kingdom of God's dear Son; but the great dragon, "that old serpent called the devil and Satan," still wears the "seven crowns [diadems] upon his heads" (Revelation xii. 3). Those diadems are the emblems of a regal authority over this world, which is not set aside till the Lamb comes forth with His "many crowns" (or diadems) on His head, and sends His angel to lay hold on the dragon, and bind him a thousand years. Rev. xii. carries us back to the woman and the serpent in Genesis iii., and the points of resemblance between the dragon in that chapter and the last beast of Revelation xiii. 1 (the final head of the Roman world) are very significant, as linking him with the temporal power of the earth. He who will give the beast "his power, and his seat [throne], and great authority," has all through the groaning ages of a world's misery given these in a greater or less degree to Nimrod, to Sennacherib, to Nebuchadnezzar, and to others afterwards; albeit God claimed them as His ministers. It is thus that the simple human form of the great image of Daniel ii., representing God's will in government,

becomes, under Satan's controlling influence, the
bestial forms of power of Daniel vii. In the former
chapter we read, " The God of heaven hath given
thee a kingdom, power, and strength, and glory ; "
in the latter we read, most significantly, " The four
winds of the heaven strove upon the great sea."
Here it is as if Satan, and not God, had the
arrangement ; and out of the storm of angry and
hateful passion came up the four great wild beasts,
fit emblems of the source whence they came, and
of him who used them as his slaves to do his will.

Truly we see Divine instruction in these things,
and heavenly distinctions, if we are prepared to
heed them. Thus we can understand Satan's
showing our Lord " all the kingdoms of the world,"
and saying to Him, " All this power [authority]
will I give to Thee, and the glory of them : for
that is delivered unto me ; and to whomsoever I
will I give it " (Luke iv. 6). The liar never lied
to the Son of God, knowing full well the lie could
have no weight with Him. Truth might influence,
and truth he told. Satan did hold a delegated
authority, and this it is he here offers ; but this
was purchased back at the Cross, and is claimed by
our Lord after His resurrection, in those ever
memorable words, " *All power* [authority] *is given
unto Me* in heaven and in earth " (Matt. xxviii. 18).
It is *given ;* but He has not as yet taken it,
nor will He till the seventh trumpet shall sound,
when it shall be said, " We give Thee thanks, O

Lord God Almighty, because Thou hast taken to
Thee Thy great power, and hast reigned." Then,
and then only, will it be true that "the kingdoms of
this world are become the kingdoms of our God,
and of His Christ" (Revelation xi. 15). Till
then the "prince of this world" rules, though his
doom was sealed at the Cross; and the Holy
Ghost, already come from heaven, testifies not only
of sin and of righteousness, but also "of judgment, because the prince of this world is judged."
The time for the execution of this judgment (*i.e.*,
the day of vengeance) has not yet come. It com-
mences with the casting out of Satan from heaven,
as seen in Revelation xii. He will then be cast
upon earth, when the time of woe to the inhabi-
tants of the world will take place, of which we
read, "Woe to the inhabiters of the earth and the
sea! for the devil is come down unto you, having
great wrath, because he knoweth that he hath
but a short time" (Revelation xii. 12). Meantime,
every spirit cast out, and we may say every soul
converted, is an earnest of the triumph that awaits
the Cross of Christ after the accomplishment of
God's purposes in the present dispensation. From
earth Satan is cast into the bottomless pit, after
the destruction of the beast and false prophet, and
their followers. There he is bound for a thousand
years, and is no longer allowed to deceive mankind till again he is loosed for a little season to
rally round him those who remained his during the

millennial reign; and then he is finally cast into
the lake of fire, where the beast and the false
prophet already are, and where all will be cast
whose names are not written in the Lamb's Book
of Life.

Satan's moral relation to man as "the god of
this age" (not "of this world") is another and
a very different subject. This he will more fully
assume when he brings in "the man of sin"
(2 Thessalonians ii. 9). Then we read: "All the
world wondered after the beast. And they worshipped the dragon" (Revelation xiii. 3, 4).

Many important practical considerations in connection with our relation to the world arise out of
the rejection of the earth's lawful King by Satan,
as the prince of this world, and the god of this
age, and these are treated of in our next article.

Satan "The God of this Age."

WE have already sought to consider the meaning of the description given by our Lord of Satan as "The prince of this world;" and we now come to a still darker page in the history of that mighty spirit, when we regard him as "The god of this age." By this title Scripture characterises the energy and working which Satan has set up, and maintains, in the face of God, over the moral and spiritual depths of man's fallen being. "If our Gospel be hid," says the apostle, "it is hid to them that are lost: in whom the god of this age [not world] hath blinded the minds of them which believe not, lest the light of the glorious Gospel of Christ, Who is the image of God, should shine unto them" (2 Cor. iv. 3, 4).

Of this "age" Paul also writes to the Ephesians, when describing their former condition as dead in trespasses and sins, "wherein in time past ye walked according to the course [*age, αιωνα*] of this world, according to [*i.e.*, in obedience to the will of] the prince of the power of the air, the spirit that now worketh in the children of disobedience." How little man dreams that his self-will and pride is none other than a flame kindled in hell, by

which he is set on fire by Satan! He thinks he is
his own master, while he is really more completely
a slave to an unseen, unknown master than ever
man was to an earthly master seen and known.

The ordinary slave has some escape and some
alleviations. There are hours and times when his
tyrant sees him not, and can affect his happiness
but little; and at length in death the slave is free
from the master. Not so in the tyranny of Satan.
His agents can always influence for evil all who
are his, and death but delivers his servants into his
hands with a more terrible certainty.

Self in the natural man is but a cover for Satan;
and whenever it asserts itself, there is behind it the
old serpent, who is God's enemy, and the enemy of
man also, as God's creature. This awful truth is
brought out in our Lord's solemn words to Peter:
" Get thee behind Me, Satan: for thou art an
offence [a cause of stumbling] unto Me: for thou
savourest not the things that be of God, but those
that be of men " (Matthew xvi. 23). Peter's word
to the Lord had been, " Be it far from Thee," or
" Pity Thyself." But whatever in us pities self,
and seeks its interest, is of man, and what is of
man is of Satan, who worketh (energiseth) in the
children of disobedience; and this, which we are
ever prone to overlook, the Son of God detected
and exposed.

The presence and power of Satanic working will
be but little recognised, except as the power of

the Spirit of God is known and felt. In these
days of growing infidelity, when "the Spirit of
Truth" and "the spirit of error" (or of the delu-
sion) are not only too often denied by unregenerate
men, but are only feebly acknowledged by too
many of God's dear children, it is of immense importance that this question be taken up in the light
of Scripture. Beyond its pages nothing is known,
or can be known, of the spirit world by which we
are surrounded, and of its mighty influence and
control over human thought and action. Because
unseen, it is unknown, and the awakenings of good,
and the stirrings of evil, are supposed to be purely
from the creature itself. The consequence of this
ignorance in the Christian is that he loses sight of
the indwelling of the Spirit of the living God,
Whose omnipotence and all-sufficiency are ever
ready to make him more than conqueror over
"manifold temptations" and trials (1 Peter i. 6),
because of the "manifold grace" (1 Peter iv. 10)
of which the blessed Spirit is the administrator.
And, on the other hand, he fails to realise that the
terrible stirrings and strivings of sin and evil in
him after his conversion, are caused by spiritual
evil agencies working on the renewed soul ; whereas
before, these corruptions were only dormant,
because unaroused by the malice of Satan. Again,
this ignorance leads unenlightened men to regard
what are really the stirrings of the Spirit of God,
as the workings of the natural love of the good

and the holy in the heart of man, as if any true light or life could burn or shine in him whom God describes as dark and dead. In other cases, the sleep of death and the peace-dream of ignorance, which the wily one seeks not to disturb, are regarded as evidences of natural goodness and piety.

This rule of Satan is one of a positive blinding and darkening power. He now blinds the minds of those that believe not, as he bound with "a spirit of infirmity eighteen years" the woman whom our Lord healed (see Luke xiii.). But in the days of the man of sin the mysteries of the present will be unfolded in the full manifestation of things as they *are*, and not as they *seem* to be; and then Satan's consummation of evil will be that all shall worship him. Now he works, not openly, but in mystery; and he seeks for worshippers, blinding them all the while as to the real object of their worship. He is thus silently preparing the world for a time when openly men will worship the beast, and worship the dragon (*i.e.*, Satan) who gave power unto the beast, saying, " Who is like unto the beast ? who is able to make war with him ?" (Revelation xiii. 4).

In the reign of Antichrist, Satan will be owned and worshipped as God (2 Thessalonians ii. 4), and this terrible unfolding to us of *the future* is given that we may read aright the mystery of *the present*. Now Satan conceals himself under the Name of the blessed God ; that which is anti-Christian is

called by the Name of Christ; the whore of
Babylon is known by the name of the Church of
God, the Bride of Christ. The Book of Revelation gives us the final form of these terrible
realities of the future, that we may see more
clearly than would otherwise be possible those
mysteries of evil by which we are now surrounded.

Satan's being "the god of this age" is, therefore, the source and the substance of this world's
idolatry, under every form of it, and by whatsoever
name it may be known, whether that idolatry be
gross or refined, whether heathen or Christian,
whether outward or inward; and hence man's
worship is called a sacrificing "to devils, and not
to God" (1 Corinthians x. 20).

In Israel's days there were novelties—"gods
that came newly up." And so it is now, for Satan
has fresh forms for all developments of human
life; and of his ways it is true, as of the ways of
the strange woman, "They are moveable, that
thou canst not [or mayest not] know them." It is
these novelties in the worship of Satan that deceive the unwary. New names, new forms, new
prophets, new christs, and new idols come up;
but the dark reality is unchanged. It is Satan
instead of God, with a greater or less measure of
the "form of godliness," the more completely to
deceive. In order to expose this, the prophetic
Word is given, so that, though specious and godly
names are used, we may not be ignorant of the

antagonism to God that underlies it all. Hence the prophetic portions of the New Testament, particularly the Book of Revelation, call for our prayerful study, if we would be wise and know the signs of the times in which we live, so as to avoid all the forms of evil which surround us.

In Babylon, Satan is god, as in Egypt Satan was king, Pharaoh's great anti-type; but He Who led us out of spiritual Egypt will lead us out of the spiritual Babylon if we are willing to be led. Our Lord is ever saying to us, " Come out of her, My people, that ye be not partakers of her sins, and that ye receive not of her plagues." This cry will be literal in the future. It is spiritual now, while " Babylon the Great " is still a " mystery " which the eye of faith alone can see, and which the spiritual mind alone will understand. To all others Babylon is that " Christendom " to which they attach the blessed Name of Christ, and which they regard as the development of the kingdom of God; but those who say, " Thy kingdom come," know it has not come, and cannot come till the King of kings shall be revealed, to execute the judgment written, according to the estimate of God, and not according to the estimate formed in " man's day."

He will then lay " judgment for the line, and righteousness for the plummet," bringing everything to the test of God's straight lines and of His unerring plummet. The hail of the wrath of God

shall then sweep away the refuges of lies, wherewith the god of this age has all along deceived the
children of the age, and, alas! has well-nigh
blinded many of the children of the age to come,
on whom, as children of the light and children of
the day, the light and the power of the coming
world, to which they belong, should have shined
with unerring clearness.

This false worship is among "the depths of
Satan, as they speak" (Revelation ii. 24); yet
these so-called "depths" are to faith the shallows
of human self-will; for to God alone belong the
depth and height, the length and breadth, of what
is real and eternal. Many phases of this idolatrous
worship are embraced in the three leavens against
which our Lord warned His disciples, and they
form the real " will-worship " which stands opposed
to the first three petitions of the prayer our Lord
taught His disciples; for this will-worship dis-
honours God, and desecrates His name, instead of
hallowing it; hinders His kingdom, instead of
advancing it; and frustrates the doing of His will
in the earth by the putting of man's will in its
place.

The three leavens that describe the spirit in
which the god of this age is worshipped are—1st,
Phariseeism. This substitutes for the commandments of God the traditions of men, and shows
itself in the ritualism of the day. It makes the
religion of man one of form and superstition, and

has in it nothing of reality, of truth, or of a living
God.   2nd, *Sadduceeism.*   This denies all that lies
beyond the grasp and the comprehension of the
creature, and makes the finite the measure of the
infinite.   We see it in all the religious free-thinking
of the day, and we hear it in the " profane and
vain babblings, and oppositions of science falsely
so called " (1 Timothy vi. 20), which proceed from
those who exchange the truth of God for the lie,
and who worship and serve the creature rather
than the Creator, Who is blessed for evermore
(Romans i. 25).   And 3rd, *Herodianism* is the hateful spirit of time-serving and of worldly conformity
that prostitutes God's things to Cæsar's use, and
profanes the hallowed things of "the Holy One
of Israel" by making them subserve the selfish
interests of human life.   The leaven of Herod
brings the Church, and its holy and heavenly
realities, into subordination to the world for its
patronage, its emoluments, and its honours.

The three leavens bring God's solemn light to
bear upon the *high*-churchism, *broad*-churchism,
and *low*-churchism, of the day, whether in the
established or non-established forms of religious
thought.   These constitute the threefold form of
man's will-worship, and they are the depths, the
mysteries of the wicked one !   The tangled thread
of six thousand years of departure from God is
alone disentangled by God's Word with perfect
distinctness.   In Revelation xvi. 13, we see the

same three forms of evil in "the three unclean spirits like frogs that come out of the mouth of the dragon [*i.e.*, Satan and spiritual wickedness], out of the mouth of the beast [*i.e.*, Cæsar, or political power], and out of the mouth of the false prophet" [*i.e.*, intellectual power and false teaching].

In conclusion, we would earnestly say to all Christians, that, bad as are the outer forms of this idolatry and will-worship, in virtual subjection to the god of this age, there is an inner working of the same that is found in the fleshly nature of every child of Adam, and has constantly to be guarded against. It forms the essential element of the unrenewed heart and the unbroken will, and those who have escaped *the outward pollution* have all the greater need to be on their guard lest they walk *in the inward corruption* of it.

Indeed, this subject has bearings which are very far-reaching, and intricacies that call for much searching of heart. Let us set ourselves to learn the length and breadth of John's last command in his first Epistle: "Little children, keep yourselves from idols"—an epistle which has an additionally solemn significance as written by him to whom the visions in the Revelation were given.

God preserve us from worshipping the prince of darkness, by enabling us ever to walk in the light, as He is in the light, and so see the trail of the serpent in what surrounds us. Then the Spirit of Truth will guide us into all truth, and preserve us from all the subtleties of the worship of "the god of this age." Let us live for the God of the age to come, " the King eternal, immortal, invisible, the only wise God," Whose Name shall be hallowed, Whose kingdom shall come, and Whose will snall be done as in heaven so on earth, when the god of this age shall be cast into the lake of fire.

God's Centre:

THE ONE NAME AND THE ONE PLACE.

IT is deeply instructive to see how God's thoughts are stereotyped in all His command-ings and in all His dispensations. The outward form may change, and external circumstances may be ever so different, but God's purposes do not change, and the believer who is wise in his reading of Old Testament teachings, reads New Testament thoughts under them, and finds that Moses, no less than Paul, bears witness to Christ.

The feasts of Israel represent certain great truths, and as in these feasts God called Israel to appear before Him, so we are called to present ourselves to God in the spiritual apprehension of these truths, and in so doing we express our allegiance to the God of Truth.

In Deuteronomy xvi., all the males in Israel were commanded to appear before the Lord three times in the year, in the *place* that He should choose. There they were called to come, and there to worship ; not in any place of their own selection, but where the Lord chose to place *His Name*, for it was the Name that gave the place its significance. The Name stands for the Person, and Paul's words in Philippians ii. emphasise this when he says that God has given to Christ "*the Name* that is above every name : that at the Name of JESUS every knee should bow, of things in heaven, and things on earth, and things under the earth." He is the Angel of God's presence, of Whom God says, "*My Name is in Him*" (Exodus xxiii. 21).

But as the Name points to Jesus, so the *place* points to Jesus, for He is the Corner-stone of the true temple, the veritable Holiest of holies, into which we are called to enter with boldness in the power of His precious blood. The Name and place are in heaven, and we need ever to remember this ; for, though we may have escaped the danger of giving sanctity to an earthly building, we may encircle our local assemblies with a heavenly halo on the ground of some outward circumstance or some pretentious creed, while the life, the power, and the glory of the heavenly reality are lacking. It is ever blessedly true that wherever two or three are gathered unto the Lord's Name, there He is, but there is more in gathering unto His Name than many suppose. Where His Name is, He is, and where He is, there is power—for with Him is the plenitude of the Spirit ; and where He is, the arm of the Lord is revealed.

Let us, then, in the holy soberness of truth, seek to dwell on the theme before us, remembering that we are never true worshippers except as we worship in spirit and in truth.

The feasts to which all Israel were to gather were three—those of the Passover, the Pentecost, and the Tabernacles ; and these point respectively to the Cross, the advent of the Holy Ghost, and the glory of the future kingdom at the marriage of the Lamb.

While meditating on these feasts and the truths they represent, may our hearts be prepared to listen to what the Lord would say to us in reference to them, for as were the feasts to Israel, so are their respective truths to us, and He who commanded Israel's attendance at the place where God had put His Name, likewise commands our fellowship at this threefold gathering place.

I. THE PASSOVER.

First, then, let us dwell a little on the Passover. The date of this feast is of special significance. It was observed in the month in which God brought His people out of Egypt. Again and again does God remind Israel of their deliverance from Pharaoh's bondage ; and so does the Spirit of God, through Paul, bid the Ephesians and all saints remember the bondage of sin and of the world, out of which all who believe are delivered by the death and resurrection of the Lord Jesus. Redemption's feast begins a new era, on the ground of which the soul can sing, " Unto Him that loveth us and washed us from our sins in His own blood," to which we can also add, " and hath made us a kingdom and priests unto His

God and Father." In memory of the deliverance
from Egypt, not only was the paschal lamb to be
slain, but burnt-offerings and peace-offerings were
also to be offered, whereby we are reminded of that
fellowship and communion with God into which we
are called in Christ Jesus. But while we are thus
shown our position and our calling on the ground
of what Christ is to us, we have, like Israel, to
partake of unleavened bread, or, as it is called here
emphatically, the "bread of affliction," which keeps
us in remembrance of our condition as sinners.
This aspect of the Cross we are prone to lose sight
of, in the joy of our salvation in Christ; and we
thus lose that fellowship in His sufferings which
the remembrance of our condition as sinners
would produce. The result of this is that we
become puffed up, rather than humbled, as we
contemplate our mighty deliverance from sin and
Satan. Against this danger God specially guards
us by the truth contained in the expression, "*bread
of affliction.*" It is added: "for ye came out of
Egypt *in haste.*" The word here rendered "haste"
implies not merely speed, but the affright and
alarm which lead to a hasty flight. The word
always implies a danger lying behind, and very
solemnly does this speak to our conscience of the
doom of Egypt, and the need of an escape like
that of Lot from Sodom.

If the power and craft of Satan were more deeply
known, the unleavened bread of sincerity and truth

would be to us the "bread of affliction." The deep experience of Romans vii. would then be better understood; sin and holiness would relatively assume vaster proportions in our minds, and the gospel of our deliverance would be more like the prophetic roll, sweet in the mouth, but bitter in the belly. May the Lord teach us this profound mystery whereby the "unleavened bread" becomes the "bread of affliction" to the soul, and enable us to understand the experience that Paul describes in 1 Corinthians ix. 24-27, which led him to keep his body under, and bring it into subjection, lest as a servant he should lose his Master's approval, or as a disciple his expected reward.

The Passover, with its deliverance and its affliction, was never to be lost sight of by Israel, for God says, "Thou shalt remember the day when thou camest forth out of the land of Egypt all the days of thy life" (Deuteronomy xvi. 3). And we are called ever to remember what we have been delivered from, as well as what we have been redeemed unto; and as we think of both, we shall walk humbly, with "fear and trembling," but also joyfully. It is deserving of notice that "affliction," rather than "joy," marks the Passover, while joy especially characterises the feasts of Pentecost and Tabernacles.

As already stated, there was only one place where the Passover could be celebrated, and that was the place which God had chosen, to put His

Name there. This is a solemn witness against man's proud independence of spirit, which would say, Any place will do, if only the spirit be right. God will have His service performed in His own way, and not in ours; and that spirit can never be right which does not seek carefully to carry out the precepts of God's Word. When, in Hezekiah's day, Israel in their haste and ignorance kept the Passover without due regard to the appointments of God, and without having cleansed themselves, the Lord smote them, though he hearkened to Hezekiah's prayer : " The good Lord pardon every one that prepareth his heart to seek God, the Lord God of his fathers, though he be not cleansed according to the purification of the sanctuary." God heard prayer and healed the people, but we have to learn that rightness of heart and motive does not justify wrong action.

The Passover, then, is our first gathering truth.

II. PENTECOST.

We now briefly consider the "*Feast of Pente-cost,*" or the "*Feast of Weeks,*" as it is generally called in the Old Testament, in its relation to the Name and the place which constituted God's centre for Israel, and around which they were called to gather in their second yearly feast.

The Passover might be held in the wilderness, but this feast could only be observed in *the land*. It was connected with the offering of the wave-sheaf on the morrow after the Sabbath following the Passover; and as the wave-sheaf points to the resurrection of Christ, so Pentecost, on which the two wave-loaves were offered, presents to us the resurrection of the Church of God; for it is as partakers of resurrection life in Christ that we are "raised up together and made to sit together in heavenly places" in Him.

This truth is essentially connected with the power of the Holy Ghost, which raises the child of God, in his new life, above the world, and makes him a citizen of heaven. It is, therefore, connected with "the land" into which by faith we are now called to enter, and to engage in the heavenly conflict, and in the power of the Holy Ghost to prove ourselves more than conquerors through Him Who loved us.

With this corresponds the experience given in Romans viii., which we have to learn out for ourselves, but our doing so will depend on the measure in which we are "led of the Spirit." It is not here a question of our being "in Christ," and of our being assured that "no condemnation" awaits us; our Passover-standing settles both these points by virtue of the precious blood of the Lamb. The question connected with the Feast of Pentecost is, as to our knowledge of the *power of the Spirit;* and this depends on us, in so far as we may grieve and hinder the Spirit's operations. All that the work of Christ effects for us is entirely

G

beyond our control, and we cannot lessen its efficacy. It is absolute, and hence our security in the new covenant is inviolable, for neither our failures nor our shortcomings affect our standing in Christ, if we are really born of God. It is thus that the "wisdom and prudence" of God's ways towards us are displayed (Ephesians i. 8). His *wisdom* makes our life absolutely sure, for it is "hid with Christ in God;" His *prudence* links the enjoyment of our spiritual blessings with our walking in the power of the Holy Ghost, and only as we so walk is our joy full, and are we perfected in love.

Hence, as has been already pointed out, the "bread of affliction" marks the Passover feast, and joy is never alluded to; while in the Pentecost, the prominent feature is *rejoicing* before the Lord; and it was not to be an individual joy, but there was to be a fellowship in it with others, reminding us of the communion of saints.

Thus Israel were commanded to gather at the Feast of Pentecost, and thus also believers are now called to gather together in the Name of the Risen Christ, and in the joy of that relationship in which we all stand before God, in the power of the Holy Ghost. On our apprehension of this precious truth, our spiritual condition depends.

"None of you shall appear before Me empty," was the command to Israel at the three feasts, but it has to be observed that this one was to be especially kept "with a tribute of a free-will offering of thine hand, which thou shalt give unto the Lord thy God according as the Lord thy God hath blessed thee." This, again, distinguishes the Pentecost from the Passover. In the latter the chief thought is that we are *receivers*, but here we are taught to bring to the Lord His tribute—a free-will offering. Thus blessings received become, according to our feeble measure, blessings returned into the bosom of our God. He hath blessed us with all spiritual blessings in Christ, and we echo the words, " Blessed be the God and Father of our Lord Jesus Christ." We loved Him because He first loved us, and to all eternity God will reap as He has sowed.

Using a comparison from Ezekiel's vision of the holy waters, which flow from under the threshold of the temple by the south side of the altar, we may say that the blessings of the Passover, which belong to the whole heavenly family, are *ankle deep*. But the Pentecostal blessings run *knee deep*, and are the portion of those who enter the land of promise, and have wherewithal to fill their basket, as they come in their worship and service to the place where the Lord has placed His Name.

III. THE FEAST OF TABERNACLES.

We have now come to " the Feast of Tabernacles," or, as it is called in Exodus xxxiv. 22, " the Feast of Ingathering." The year rolls on, and the closing feast arrives. So God's dispensations roll on, one following another, until, in figure, we reach the final stage—the glory of the kingdom, and the feast of heavenly joy at the marriage of the Lamb. Then, with hallowed memories of the past, we shall sit down under the bridal canopy of the blessings of the eternal covenant, and prove that nothing has failed of all that God has spoken, and, indeed, that the half had not been told.

At this last feast all Israel were to assemble; and *we* are called to gather in the precious hope of the coming glory, and even now by faith to enter into it, though in fact it is still future. Thus we have presented to us the *third* truth connected with the one name and the one place, namely, the glory to be revealed when the Lord shall come and receive us unto Himself. The light of the second advent is made to shine out upon our daily path, and we learn what it is to be " saved in hope," a hope sure and certain, because it enters into that within the veil, for a Risen Christ at the right hand of God is the pledge to us of a coming Christ, Who will gather His people into the place He has gone to prepare. In connection with this feast, as with Pentecost, comes the command, " Thou shalt rejoice;" and, as if to make this command doubly strong, it is repeated, " Thou shalt *surely* rejoice," or " Thou shalt be *altogether* joyful " (R.V.)

Let us now turn to Nehemiah viii., which may prove a word in season to some in whose experience the joy of the future is clouded and overshadowed by the trials of the present.

In the days in which Nehemiah lived and laboured, the children of Israel were in weakness, oppression, and sorrow. Sanballat, Tobiah, Geshem, and others, were doing their worst, while half-hearted Israelites and treacherous nobles greatly added to the perplexities, the difficulties, and sorrows of that time; but this chapter brings us to the feast of the seventh month, and it will be well for us to ponder the blessed record of it.

The law of God had been read, and where conscience was alive, there could but be mourning and tears; hence we read that "all the people wept when they heard the words of the law." But note God's word to them through His servant Nehemiah (whose name means "The consolation of Jehovah"): "Go your way, eat the fat, and drink the sweet, and send portions unto them for whom nothing is prepared, for this day is holy unto the Lord; neither be ye sorry, for the joy of the Lord is your strength" (verse 10).

In these tender, loving words, from the very heart of our God, the lesson He would teach us is, that while it is well for eyes to weep, and for hearts to be sad at the failure which His Word, if read with understanding, must reveal, it is essential for His glory, and for our blessing, that we should never allow our failures to eclipse in our souls the sense of the sure accomplishment of the eternal

purposes of God, and the joy that springs from
the assurance of their final realisation. *The victory
is His*, even though the Sanballats and Tobiahs of
this day, the half-hearted fellow-Christians, the
treacherous rulers and nobles, the false prophets,
and lying prophetesses, all combine against the
cause of God, His truth and His Word. Let us
keep this ever in mind, and because the victory is
His, it is also ours, and we can sing through our
many sorrows,

> " The victory is ours ;
> For us in might came forth the Mighty One ;
> For us He fought the fight, the triumph won ;
> The victory is ours."

Surely there is fatness to be eaten, and sweetness to be drunk, by all who truly know what our
feast of love is ! " Consolation in Christ," " comfort of love," " fellowship of the Spirit," and
" bowels and mercies," may still be enjoyed by
those whose " citizenship is in heaven ;" and to
this we would direct all hearts, that they may find
" the joy of the Lord " to be their " strength "
and their sufficiency for all present need.

Here, then, is *our* third great gathering truth,
which tells us at the Lord's table that we show
forth His death " *till He come*." " Till He come "
we are down here, and when He comes we shall
be up yonder.

In conclusion, we would reiterate some points
connected with the command in Deuteronomy xvi.
16, 17: " Three times in the year shall all thy

males appear before the Lord thy God in the place
which He shall choose." Earnestly would we
press upon our fellow-believers this point—that
if we would know our calling in Christ Jesus and
walk worthy of it, if we would attain the full
stature of manhood in Christ, our faith must lay
hold of (1) the Passover truth of the redeeming
power of the blood of Christ; (2) the Pentecostal
truth of the resurrection power of the Holy Ghost;
and (3) the truth set forth in the Feast of Tabernacles concerning the future glory and triumph of
the Son of God. While, however, all these truths
are essential to him who desires to be "an Israelite
indeed," "a man in Christ," a distinction has to
be drawn as to the necessity of their being equally
apprehended. While the command of Deut. xvi.
16, 17, includes the *three* feasts, there is an *im-
perativeness* connected with the Passover which
does not extend to the other two feasts, and in our
zeal for the truth this must not be lost sight of.
Of the Passover it is said that "the man that is
clean, and is not in a journey, and forbeareth to
keep the Passover, even the same soul *shall be cut
off* from among his people : because he brought
not the offering of the Lord in its appointed
season, that man shall bear his sin" (Num. ix. 13).
Thus, while every Israelite was commanded to
come to all three feasts, it was only absence from
the Passover that would sever him from the people
of God.

We are living in days when advanced truths are being applied as *necessary* to the fellowship of the Israel of God, but while we would yield to none in maintaining the absolute claim God has on our obedience, and our responsibility to have one mind and one mouth concerning the hallowed truths indicated in the feasts before us, yet we are bound to add that we have no authority to separate from our fellowship children of God who, so to speak, neglect to come to the feasts of Pentecost and Tabernacles; though they thereby disobey God, and wrong their own souls by this neglect of His truth. It was God, and God only, Who had power to say who should, and who should not, be within the camp of His people; and now it is Christ, and Christ only, Who has the power to exclude from His assemblies; and He Who "hates putting away," and would have us regard it as the cutting off of our own right hand, or the plucking out of our right eye, will not justify a discipline He has not enjoined, or the excision of disobedient believers whom He has not commanded us to exclude. To his own Master each believer stands or falls, and in such matters, if he will not heed our counsel from God's Word, we must leave him to be dealt with by Christ at His judgment-seat, and see to it that we set him an example of obedience, of lowliness, and of love.

There are moral and spiritual apostasies for which we have to exclude even a brother; and

there are other unseemly matters for which we
have to withhold the intimacy of private fellowship, as in 2 Thessalonians iii. 12, 14, but in
reference to which we can go no further. The
sons of Levi took too much upon them in more
ways than one, but as surely as they did so, judgment followed. We have seen the judgment of
God fall upon false systems of discipline—false
because not appointed of God ; and may God give
to us, His servants, lowlier hearts, and enable us
to walk with gentler footsteps in His Church, and
to think more of obedience in ourselves, than of
disobedience in others.

Another point touched on here is, " They shall
not appear before the Lord empty: every man
shall give as he is able, according to the blessing
of the Lord thy God which He hath given thee."
We would remind our fellow-believers of the claim
the Lord has on us, both in spiritual and in
temporal things. Let us give as He has given.
Let the precious stream of spiritual and temporal
good flow on.

> " Let the tide of blessing roll
> Far and wide, from pole to pole—
> Blessing deep, exhaustless, free,
> Bringing glory, Lord, to Thee."

To let it stagnate in our souls, or in our coffers, is
to turn God's blessings into curses. Alas! for the
stagnant truth, the stagnant grace, the stagnant
strength, the stagnant money, to be found in the

Church of God! May it roll on, so that each blessed one may be made a blessing in his turn.

The Lord bless this chapter, and the reflections it suggests, to us all in Christ Jesus, according to the need of each one.

"Living Hope" and "Joy Unspeakable."

OUR joy should ever be in God Himself, and not in anything He gives us. Ours would then be a rejoicing pilgrimage, and we should not be found groaning over the thorns of the wilderness, and dwelling upon the difficulties and trials of the way; but our thoughts would be full of the omnipotence of God, and of the shelter of His outstretched wings. God did not remind Israel of the thorns, but of His promises, of His grace and love, of the pillar and cloud, of the manna, and of the water from the smitten rock.

We shall never know the Cross until we have borne it. One peculiar characteristic of the Church of God is, that we are not saved out of the sphere of sorrow, but inside it; and this makes the fellowship of the Church so much nearer to Christ, a nearness that the angels are unacquainted with. I am not aware that the fellowship of angels in the sphere of sorrow is ever named in connection with God; but *we* have a partnership of faith in the Cross and in the glory. "If we suffer, we shall also reign with Him." If we enter into this, then bereavements will lose much of their weight, and

we shall know the power of the Divine antidote
for sorrow, given in 1 Thessalonians iv., concerning which Paul says: "Wherefore comfort one
another with these words."

To follow up these thoughts, let us turn to the
opening words of Peter's First Epistle.

*"Blessed be the God and Father of our Lord
Jesus Christ."* We are blessed in God, but do we
realise how blessed God is in us? We scarcely
understand the surface meaning of such words,
to say nothing of their hidden depths. A blessed
people with a blessed God! Not one of us is going
to be disappointed. A thousandth part has not
been told. We shall be satisfied; and shall Christ
be dissatisfied concerning us? "He shall see of
the travail of His soul, and shall be satisfied."
These are wonderful things to read and speak of.
Let us open our hearts to let in the love that all
these blessings imply. More wonderful is it to
think of the Hand that gives them to poor, condemned sinners. Let the most tried child of God
realise how blessed he is, and how blessed God is
in him, and sorrow will turn to joy.

"Who hath begotten us again unto a living hope."
Our regeneration is unto a purpose that lies beyond.
There is a joy, a bliss, now; but it leads to something far greater hereafter. When we stand by
the graves of our loved ones, and our tears are
falling, it is well to look right up into heaven and
think of our "living hope" there. May God write

in large letters that joyful, living, sustaining word
HOPE. It has arms to it, and will embrace us in
its joy.

"*By the resurrection of Jesus Christ from the
dead.*" It is this that gives to us the hope. The
Cross began the work of our salvation, but the
resurrection was the consummation of it, its seal
and pledge. What a contrast between the tabernacle and the builded house! (2 Corinthians v. 1.)
The pins of the tabernacle are soon taken up, and
the cords are easily loosed. One letter tells us of
a *tent* beginning to shake, and another comes to
say the tent is down. But in blessed contrast is
the eternal perpetuity of the *house* that lies beyond.
As we think of this, and know that the tent *must*
come down, we are tempted to say: "The sooner
the better." But not so; we have lessons to learn
here which cannot be learned there. Rather let
us increasingly value the instruction which God is
patiently bestowing on us by means of the trials,
toils, and difficulties of the wilderness.

"*To an inheritance incorruptible.*" In the midst
of earth's poor, transient possessions, let us dwell
on the character of our inheritance. "Incorruptible" is a word which Peter loves to use. In
contrast with corruptible "silver and gold," he
places "the precious blood of Christ," and God's
Word in contrast with man's—"born again, not of
corruptible seed, but of incorruptible, by the Word
of God, which liveth and abideth for ever." The

"meek and quiet spirit," as that which is incorruptible within, is also set over against all the outward fading adornments. May we learn, amidst the corruptions of time, the incorruptibility of the eternal kingdom to which we are hastening.

"*Undefiled.*" It cannot be contaminated. It is said of our Lord in the Revelation that His feet were of burnished brass, implying that He walked undefiled amidst the defilements of the churches. Where defilement is, corruption follows; but our inheritance is incorruptible, and nothing that defileth can enter it. Let us seek in this respect to be more in keeping with our inheritance.

"*And that fadeth not away.*" It is not like the flowers of earth, which are cut down and cast into the oven. The beautiful sun rises and sets, and sunsets fade and darken into night; vanity is written upon everything here; but we are going to a place where there is no withering and no fading.

"*Reserved in heaven for you.*" The use of this word *reserved* in Peter's Second Epistle may well remind us of the mercy that secures the inheritance for us. There we read of "judgment" reserved for angels that sinned, and for the unjust, and of the "blackness of darkness" reserved for those who are the servants of corruption.

"*Who are kept by the power of God.*" "Your life is hid with Christ in God." Nobody can touch it, for we are bound up in the bundle of life with the Lord. We are "guarded" as by a garrison.

"The angel of the Lord encampeth round about them that fear Him, and delivereth them" (Psalm xxxiv. 7).

Elisha prays for his servant that his eyes may be opened, and then he sees chariots of fire and horses of fire (2 Kings vi. 17). May we get Dothan revelations to our own souls! If it were not for the eye that sees all the dangers that lie before us, and for the guarding by holy angels, how should we do when the hosts of hell are engaged against us? But we are "kept by the power of God."

"*Through faith.*" The stronger our faith is, the greater will be our assurance and our joy.

"*Unto salvation, ready to be revealed.*" Not ready to be possessed by us, but awaiting an unfolding by-and-bye. "Now are we the sons of God, and it doth not yet appear what we shall be" (1 John iii. 2). Present circumstances cannot affect what we are, but what we are cannot now be manifested. In our own present sense of weakness, we are waiting for the "moment" of rapture, and joy, and bliss, and love.

"*Wherein ye greatly rejoice, or exult.*" Exultation is a bursting joy; not the quiet stillness of rejoicing, but that which cannot be kept in—our hearts full, our lips full, our souls full. Oh, how little of this exultation of joy there is in our hearts!

"*Though now for a season, if need be, ye are in heaviness.*" Peter knew how hard and bitter chastening is; he recalls it here; the exultation needs to be qualified by an *if.* If there is "*manifold temptation,*" there is also "manifold grace." Ye are kept "through faith," says the apostle, but there must be "*the trial of your faith.*" Let us not fear the sorrows, the trials, the fire by which our faith is tested. Faith will have its full approval "*at the appearing of Jesus Christ.*"

"*Whom having not seen, ye love.*" The apostle recalls the Lord's words to Thomas, as to the blessedness of those who have not seen and yet have believed. He had himself seen the Lord after the resurrection, and in answer to His thrice-repeated question had said: "Thou knowest that I *love* Thee;" and here he unites in this same love those who had not seen and yet had believed.

"*Ye rejoice* [exult] *with joy unspeakable and full of glory.*" Even in the "*salvation*" (verse 5) there is exultation, but in the *Saviour* the exultation is with a joy that cannot be told out, and that anticipates the glory. May God teach us more of the love that leads to this exceeding joy, so that, come what may, the living hope may ever inspire our souls. May the Holy Spirit open our eyes, ears, and hearts, and may these words be to us what they were to the holy man who wrote them.